"Through his masterful storytelling Father Nigel Mumford offers insight into the devastating effects of extreme trauma on the human life and helps us to understand this condition known as PTSD or Post Traumatic Stress Disorder. Nigel shares candid accounts from his own traumatic experiences and from the stories of the many people he has come in contact with over the years. What sets this book apart is the transforming power of hope and the healing that occurs when people reach beyond themselves."

Jan Benjamin Janice Guay Benjamin,
Licensed Master Social Worker

"This valuable and faith inspiring book is Fr. Nigel's best yet. Although other's stories of trauma and healing are significant, it is Fr. Nigel's own testimony of many of the most traumatic events of his life that makes this book a manual of healing. This book is an invaluable 'must have' for anyone suffering from trauma or ministering healing in the military, with first responders or for those that care for them."

Lt. Col. Noel Dawes
British Army, Ret

"My Christian brother and fellow Royal Marine has written a book born from his own deep experience of trauma and pain and his healing relationship with the loving compassionate Christ. Much of Nigel's past pain was caused by his experiences in my own homeland of Northern Ireland and for me it is immensely touching to see how God has redeemed these experiences. I have had the privilege first hand of seeing and experiencing the Lord working through Nigel to "unchain" those experiencing PTSD. This book, I am sure, will be a real encouragement both to those living with trauma and those who wish to be used to help release them. In these days when incidents of trauma for those in my own country's armed forces and their loved ones is sadly increasing. I pray that it would be widely read by all involved in trauma ministry and that the Lord would be seen to work through it."

Colonel Jos McCabe OBE
Chief Executive and Team Leader,
Military Ministries International

"Fr. Nigel is no stranger to trauma; in fact, you could say it's become a kind of life companion, strange as that may seem. He's experienced the terrors of war, an almost fatal accident, and a life-threatening physical assault upon his body. And he constantly experiences the pain and sorrow as witness to the unimaginable suffering of the hundreds who have walked through his door seeking hope and healing.

This book is written with clarity, tenderhearted openness, and yes, even humor. Fr. Nigel has breathed life into the phenomenon that is Post-Traumatic Stress, making it tangible, palpable, and visceral. I believe this should be required reading for all therapists."

Abigail Brenner, MD,
psychiatrist and author of Transitions: How Women Embrace
Change and Celebrate Life *and*
SHIFT: How to Deal When Life Changes

Father Nigel Mumford understands post-traumatic stress as a result of his military experience! His passion to bring understanding and healing is evident in his writing. As a military chaplain for over thirty years, I know firsthand the devastation that traumatic stress can cause. Post-Traumatic Stress Disorder is not a new phenomenon. Historical references of PTSD are centuries old. What is new is that we now recognize PTSD and treat the disorder. I thank God for Father Mumford and his healing ministry!

Chaplain Major General (ret) John B Ellington Jr
USAF

AFTER THE TRAUMA
TRAUMA

THE BATTLE
BEGINS

Post Trauma Healing

Nigel W. D. Mumford

Cover and book design by The Troy Book Makers

Printed in the United States of America
The Troy Book Makers • Troy, New York
www.thetroybookmakers.com

To order additional copies of this title,
contact your favorite local bookstore.

ISBN: 978-1-61468-024-6

DEDICATION

This book is dedicated to my dear wife, Lynn, who has walked this path of life and near death with me. She has pulled me through so much and has learned how to live with me during the process of healing from PTSD and the disabilities caused by H1N1. It was Lynn who shouted at me, while I was in a coma, and so close to death, "Do not leave me!" Thank you to Megan for standing by my bed and being there for her mum and for me. Thank you to Matthew who flew in from California to help his mum and me, while I was floating in the heavens!

In memory of my good pal and dear friend, Col. William Quayle, Royal Artillery, UK, who after 38 years of smoking, asked me to tell people: "Please don't smoke!"

To The Rt. Rev David Bena, Col. Noel Dawes and Sandra Lester (who kept telling me to continue with the WHI even when I did not want to) for their dedicated help in the "Welcome Home Initiative."

To the men and women of the armed forces of the United States of America and the United Kingdom.

To the lads of 41 and 42 Commando Royal Marines and the Drill instructors at the Commando Training School Lympstone, Devon. UK.

ACKNOWLEDGMENTS

A huge thank you goes to my dear friend and mentor, The Rt. Rev. David Bena, who bluntly told me, Marine to Marine, to get writing this book! That is not quite what he said but its close enough! Bishop Dave, thank you for the many hours spent editing. Thank you also to Cindi Sholander for spending countless hours in research and mastering the words to help bring this book to publication. Thank you Sister Mary Jean for the final edit.

I thank my dear family who could not be with me during my sickness. I am so grateful to my brother, Alec, who flew to the USA twice from England while I was in a coma. I am so sorry that we couldn't talk to each other at the time, but thanks for poking me in the ankles and telling me to wake up! I did... eventually!

A huge thank you goes to Beth Strickland who kept everyone informed via the internet in how to pray accurately for me. Those prayers worked! I thank the thousands of people all over the world who prayed for me in 2009, while I was near death from H1N1 swine flu; especially The Rt. Rev. William Love, The Rev. Chip Strickland, The Rev. Joe Caron, the Rev. John Hopkins and The Rev. Lynn Curtis and all the clergy of the Albany diocese. The staff of Christ the King Spiritual Life Center, Greenwich NY and the peoples of the Episcopal Diocese of Albany, A U.S. Marine unit in Afghanistan, a U.S. Army unit in Iraq. Thanks to the vicar of Baghdad, Canon Andrew White and the children of St. George's, Baghdad (who even threw a party when I left the hospital. See the last page of "Suffer the Children" by Andrew White) and all those who remained connected in prayer for me through the internet. I want to honor the memory of four of my friends who died while serving with me in the Royal Marines as well as those who were injured either in body or mind from combat related injuries. Thank you to John Hyde and his staff at Prime Care, a huge help to us during my rehab at home. A huge thank you, beyond words, to the doctors and nurses of Saratoga Hospital and Sunnyview rehab hospital. A special thank you to Tasha and Karen, my ICU nurses at Saratoga and to my OT's , Julie and Tom, at Sunnyview. You are amazing people. A huge thank you to the doctors who saved my life: Dr. Carlos Ares, Dr. Rodney Ying and Dr. Desmond Delgiacco. Thank you Dr. Austin Tsai, my GP, for your dedicated help to Lynn and me during my illness and the recovery process. Thank you all so very much.

To all victims traumatized by combat experiences at home or abroad. God bless you all.

Contents

FOREWORD

General the Lord Dannatt GCB CBE MC,
DLChief of the General Staff,
British Army, 2006-2009

There are few people that one meets in life who have confronted death as starkly as Nigel Mumford has, and who can then describe their experiences for the benefit of others as he has done. This book is a remarkable testament to the triumph of spiritual healing over the despair of illness—physical or mental, real or imagined, or perhaps an amalgam of all four. For Nigel Mumford these things are not theoretical, they are his practical experience and therefore his testimony is all the more authentic because he writes about what he knows and promotes what he believes—nothing can be more genuine.

As terrible as the physical injuries of war or a horrific accident can be, the sufferer rarely has to explain his or her condition to others as the scars are plain to see. But more numerous and more painful are those whose injuries are invisible, and for them there is the additional challenge of persuading others of the existence of their problem, and its severity. Quite properly Nigel Mumford subtitles this book: "After the Ordeal, the Battle begins..." It is this ordeal—experienced by so many over the years, but unrecognised by so many for far too long—that is the focus of this book. In the pages that follow he traces the history of our understanding of Post-Traumatic Stress Disorder, describes its characteristics and its consequences and places the condition as an everyday reality both in war abroad and in the supposed peace of life at home.

Nigel Mumford's journey of understanding, explanation and healing through the pages of this book is underpinned by scriptural authority and inspirational experience. The combination is effective and compelling. However, the reader is not just left with a warm feeling of hope but instead given a spiritual and practical life plan based around seven carefully argued and explained steps. So this book is both a thriller to the opening chapter Nigel Mumford quotes extensively from Psalm 121. This psalm of inspiration, bidding us to "lift up mine eyes unto the hills from whence comes my help" is well known and well placed here but I would draw out a further thought from within its verses. In the King James Version, the last two verses read:

"The Lord shall preserve thee from all evil: he shall preserve thy soul. The Lord shall preserve thy going out and thy coming in from this time forth, and even for evermore."

How many times have prayers been offered to preserve "thy going out and coming in" on behalf of those in military combat, or even in the mundane daily round of civilian life, only to result in death, physical injury or mental scarring? How does that loving God allow these things to take place when the psalmist states that "The Lord shall preserve thee from all evil"?

Nigel Mumford answers this most critical dilemma in life through the pages of this book. The truth that he seeks to explain is that our physical bodies, though important for a while as we live our earthly lives, have no value in the grand order of things. What matters is not our physical or even mental health in this life, but the health of our soul – our inner being – that intangible part of us that is immortal for good or ill. The psalmist is unequivocal: "he (the Lord) shall preserve thy soul". It is our soul, not our bodies, that really matters and a soul dedicated to the service of Almighty God is a soul that is eternally healthy, free from physical or mental injury, and it is that which will be preserved "even for evermore."

So this book is first and last a book of hope. Towards the end, Nigel Mumford reverts to discussion of the "Welcome Home" initiative, that most important but often confusing experience for the returning veteran. He exhorts the reader: "Be well, do good works, and for the sake of God, love one another." But the homecoming that really matters is the greeting for the Christian soldier when one day, after a lifetime of service, he hears the words of St Matthew Chapter 25, verse 21:"Well done, good and faithful servant."

Now read on, and be truly encouraged.

Richard Dannatt

MINISTERING TO A FRIEND IN DIRE STRAITS

by Bishop David Bena

2009-2010 were difficult years for Nigel Mumford, his dear wife Lynn, his staff, the many people who made up his healing and prayer teams, and the thousands of people who received preaching, teaching and healing from his ministry. But they were particularly difficult for my wife Mary Ellen and me. We had been ministering alongside Nigel during the heady days of 2003-2009, days when Nigel was strong and effective, as he was an instrument of healing in the lives of so many. So it was very particularly challenging for us to see him at death's door in the hospital bed in late 2009. Here was the one who brought healing to so many, now in need of radical healing in his own right. We visited at the hospital often with him, with Lynn, and with his faithful assistant Sandra. We joined others in anointing him, praying for him, and encouraging him. We just knew that any day he would start getting better. But as he slipped into a coma, getting worse day by day, I began to wonder whether he would pull out of it. Of course, I had to be strong and encouraging. But I kept wondering to myself and to God, "Will he get better, Lord? Is there really anything to this healing business or is it just mind over matter?" We get belted with doubts when a loved one's life is threatened, don't we? So I had to push through the doubts and continue praying. There is a phrase, "Hope for the best; plan for the worst." MARY ELLEN AND I PRAYED FOR THE BEST AND PLANNED FOR THE WORST. The worst came one night when Sandra texted to say that the doctor had told Lynn not to leave the hospital that night because it would likely be Nigel's last. We drove immediately to the hospital where I administered the Last Rites to him, AFTER I asked God to completely heal him. As I said goodbye to him, part of me thought that that would be the last time I would see Nigel alive on the earth. The next day he was still alive. And the next. And the next. Time seemed in suspension as we checked on him each day. Then he began to rally. Eventually he was brought out of the coma.

Eventually he was able to talk, and then to walk, and then to begin praying for others again. Today, over one year after he got ill, he is again ministering full time. A miracle! What did we all learn from Nigel's illness? "Pray for the best; plan for the worst." The bishops, clergy, and lay people who sustained Nigel in prayer know that God is indeed in control of the universe, that He loves us all very much, and that He wants to heal us. Some will be healed immediately, some eventually, and some will be healed after they have ceased to live on the earth. Ours is to pray fervently and watch for God to act.

The Rt. Rev David Bena
Vietnam Veteran

Notes from the Author

The author's personal description of PTSD:

The mind is witness to a catastrophic event.
The intellect cannot cope with what it has seen.
The body reacts physically under duress.
The heart receives emotional scar tissue.
The soul weeps.
This mental trauma is a total body reaction to horror.

Be kinder than necessary—
Everyone you meet is fighting some kind of battle.
Anonymous

In war, there are no unwounded soldiers!
Jose Narosky

This book is written for Post-Traumatic Stress Disorder (PTSD) sufferers and for their loved ones. PTSD is a type of anxiety disorder. It can occur after you've seen or experienced a traumatic event that involved the threat of injury or death, yours or others. It includes but is not limited to such events as rape, military combat and war-related concerns, suicide, violent personal assault, robbery, muggings, kidnapping, being taken hostage, torture, incarceration as a prisoner of war or in a concentration camp, natural or manmade disasters, murder, riots, severe automobile accidents, being diagnosed with a life-threatening illness, an airplane crash, a falling building, a bomb blast, random shootings, school bullying, abuse, sexual abuse, gang violence, and acts of terrorism, or unexpectedly witnessing a dead body or body parts.

Section 309.81 of the DSM-IV (Diagnostic and Statistical Manual of Mental Disorders, fourth edition) sets forth the current official clinical diagnosis of PTSD and is readily accessible on the internet.

All verses from the Holy Bible contained herein are taken from the New International Version (©1984) translation, unless otherwise specifically indicated.

For the Warrior:

When you go to war against your enemies and see horses and chariots and an army greater than yours, do not be afraid of them, because the LORD your God, who brought you up out of Egypt, will be with you.

Deuteronomy 20:1

For trauma suffered within your family:

Now Cain said to his brother Abel, "Let's go out to the field." And while they were in the field, Cain attacked his brother Abel and killed him.

Genesis 4:8

For family members and care givers:

So do not fear, for I am with you; do not be dismayed, for I am your God. I will strengthen you and help you; I will uphold you with my righteous right hand.

Isaiah 41:10

PREFACE

Beginning in October 2009, I faced yet another battle for my life while in the intensive care unit of Saratoga Hospital. Everyone thought I was dying. I wasn't given a vote in the matter since I was in a coma at the time. By God's grace I survived and am now living to tell my story.

I was allowed to come home just before Christmas 2009. Not long afterwards, my wife, Lynn, and I adopted a puppy. He has such energy and humor, and is so full of life and everything about life! He runs about so happy and inquisitive with everything about life and living. Having survived my recent brush with death, since returning home I now sign off my emails with, "It is soooooooooo good to be alive!" Our puppy is the epitome of life from God. I see a parallel between my newly restored wonder at being alive and the unrestrained enthusiastic way Sir Duncan doggie loves life. I feel as though I am experiencing new life through the eyes of my new best friend.

I recently spoke with a grandparent, a former Gunnery Sergeant of the U.S. Marine Corps. He had just taken his grandchildren to Disney World, and though he'd been there many times before, he experienced it anew and afresh. His perspective was changed as he looked at everything through his grandchildren's eyes of wonder, joy and excitement. That's how I felt as I emerged from the valley of the shadow of death.

This book will provide very personal insight into the sufferings of the mind, body, and soul in the days, months, and years following the trauma of combat. These combat zones may include wars fought in the home—childhood terror memories; wars abroad—the horrors of military battle; and wars of survival—trauma from life-threatening illness. All traumas can lead to suffering from what is diagnosed as Post Traumatic Stress Disorder (PTSD). The symptoms of PTSD are triggered by terrifying life experiences in the theater of war, in the mind, at home, or in the supposed safety of a child's bedroom. PTSD can also result from childhood exposure to combative or abusive parents, siblings, extended family members, as well as neighbors and babysitters.

First responders, those in the business of rescuing people, such as firefighters, emergency medical technicians, and police, are also potential victims of PTSD. Since trauma can be imprinted in the mind by witnessing another's life being threatened with death, first responders are frequently troubled by what they encountered at the scene of an accident or natural disaster. I pray that this book will help those who have been traumatized to understand what has happened to them and to be encouraged that they do not have to continue to live in fear. I also pray that this book will help those who care for sufferers of PTSD to feel less stressed and guilty as they nurture their hurting loved ones. My hope in writing is that PTSD victims, and those who care for them, will become aware and grab hold of the process of healing from trauma and will give themselves grace as they battle to regain their right minds and their ability to live in freedom.

PTSD is not new. Our understanding of it continues to evolve, but this disorder has been a scourge on mankind since Creation. I never cease to be amazed at the evidence of its historic existence that popped up as I wrote this book. I found a moving quote carved on the north entrance of the DuPont Circle metro stop in Washington, D.C. Written in 1865 and taken from Walt Whitman's poem "The Wound Dresser" as contained in his book, *Leaves of Grass*, the massive engraving reads: *Thus in silence in dreams' projections, Returning, resuming, I thread my way through the hospitals; The hurt and wounded I pacify with soothing hand, I sit by the restless all dark night—some are so young; Some suffer so much—I recall the experience sweet and sad...* Whitman nursed Civil War wounded soldiers as they fell in battle. Those are the verses quoted on a wall in D.C., but in the poem's entirety, they are preceded by these revealing words penned by the traumatized poet: *I dress the perforated shoulder, the foot with the bullet-wound, Cleanse the one with a gnawing and putrid gangrene, so sickening, so offensive, while the attendant stands aside me holding the tray and pail. I am faithful, I do not give out, The fractured thigh, the knee, the wound in the abdomen, These and more I dress with "impassive hand" (yet deep in my breast a fire, a burning flame).* By his words, impassive hand, Whitman discloses his numbed feelings. *Yet the impression of impassivity is negated by words that immediately follow, yet deep in my breast a fire, a burning flame.* Could Walt Whitman have suffered from PTSD?

It is possible. When PTSD victims shut down, they appear void of all emotion and expression, but all the while they conceal a simmering fury deep within them. My purpose in sharing much of my personal story and struggles with PTSD is to help you and your loved ones come to a new way of thinking. I know that you can live again and be freed from a cloud of depression and revulsion that may yet be following you around since witnessing some horror. I believe that if you ask God to "push the reset button of the mind," you will discover a place where memories no longer control your life. The power of your assailant, whether a perpetrator, an illness, or your past, can be diffused by healing. As I understand it, in Luke 4:18-19,

Jesus tells us that He came to set the captives free. PTSD victims are captives. I know because He freed me! This book will be a resource to bring you into the healing that I have experienced and which I am privileged to help countless others to attain. Though we cannot unlearn an experience, we can be healed as the memories of our past are put in order, and processed, and peace is restored.

Fr. Nigel+

CHAPTER ONE

The Loch Ness Monster

I lift up my eyes to the hills—
where does my help come from?
My help comes from the LORD,
the Maker of heaven and earth.

Psalm 121:1-2

I *lift up my eyes to the hills—where does my help come from?* For many years after my combat experience, lifting my eyes to the hills translated to…" Where is the sniper hiding?" My mind constantly considered all the possibilities of where danger was lurking. I was hyper-vigilant, looking for the entrenched enemy, on guard at all times. "As I lift my eyes to the hills where is the pain going to come from?" Even closing the curtains at night, I imagined a looming threat. Reaching my hands out, just as Jesus did as He was crucified, I would grab at the drapes … my inner voice shouting, "Okay, shoot me now—wherever you are hiding!" These were the constant reminders of my emotional wounds from combat.

Today, the words of Psalm 121 give me such comfort as I look out my window every morning into the hills. At night when the sky is clear, I always see three lights, as though the Trinity is watching over me. I smile every time I see it. Not a bad way to begin and end each day! I now know where my help comes from: The Lord, the Maker of heaven and earth!

The origin of Psalm 121 comes from the locals of Bhael

who left the city to erect altars to false gods in the hills, outside of the city. The psalmist is saying that he's reminded that his help does not come from the false gods in the hills but from the one and only true God who made heaven and earth. Psalm 121:3-8 continues: *He will not let your foot slip —he who watches over you will not slumber; indeed, he who watches over Israel will neither slumber nor sleep. The Lord watches over you – the Lord is your shade at your right hand; the sun will not harm you by day, nor the moon by night. The Lord will keep you from all harm – he will watch over your life; the Lord will watch over your coming and going both now and forevermore.* This Psalm makes a good prayer when the trigger of post-traumatic stress disorder (PTSD) is pulled.

Psalm 121 reminds me of a visit to "bonny Scotland" many years ago. I had gone to Arbroath and started the journey back to England taking the "high road" (the long way home), driving up the east coast and then returning down the center of the country. It was early morning. The mist was hanging; the drizzle was wet on the car's windshield. The occasional glimpse of rolling hills framed in fog captured the beauty of Scotland. "Oh God, from where is my help to come?" I stopped the car next to a well-known loch. Getting out, I was struck by the wonderful smell of the bracken, the dew attached to everything God made. The damp cold went right to my bones.

I could see, but it was more like tunnel vision as the mist hung like a blanket, hiding the sniper positions I imagined. "Was I safe in this cocoon?" I wandered down to the water—the very edge of the famed Loch Ness. My heart was pounding. I could no longer see my car and felt very alone. "Thump, thump," as if the sound of my heartbeat was loudly ricocheting off the loch itself. I stood at the water's edge and looked into its darkness. "Am I being watched?" My imagination ran wild, Hollywood kicked into gear and the soundtrack from Jaws began to stream through my mind: "dah-dum…dah-dum…dah-dum." "I am alone with the Loch Ness monster, is he watching me?" I walked briskly (no I confess, I ran) back to the car, looking over my shoulder many times. "What is the 'monster' in my mind? *What* am I running from?" The Bottom Line: the threat of death…real or perceived!

I have been involved in the healing ministry of Jesus Christ since 1990 and have prayed with many as "monsters"… real or perceived, were unpacked. I've encountered so many people with baggage and horrors from the past. They need to be healed, reframed, put right. Many are lost in the deep waters of darkness, lost in the wilderness of emotional disorders: fear, terror, dread, horror, anxiety, apprehension, nervousness, depression, obsessions, addictions, torment, self-medications (alcohol, drugs, etc.), and all sorts of temptations. The play button of the mind's DVD can be pushed by all kinds of triggers, all types of "monsters' roaming about the brain! The mind can be a wilderness of terrible torment. I am told this by others regularly. And for several years I, too, suffered torment—real or perceived— from the trauma and aftermath of combat.

Though I've had many years to reflect on what happened during that period of my life from 1972-1974, memories flood my mind even as I write this. I arrived in the city of Belfast as a Royal Marine two months after Bloody Sunday. The internal and unspoken tensions of policing the streets were palpable. I was a walking target, cannon fodder, waiting for that bullet with my name on it. I can vividly remember those months of visual, emotional and physical trauma as I witnessed man's inhumanity to man. Mankind can be so cruel. Man*kind?* I would at this time of my life reframe that as man-*unkind*. I felt the immense anxiety of waiting for the result of a bullet that I wouldn't even hear.

"Where would it hit—my head, my arm, my heart? What would it feel like? Would I even feel it?" I was hounded by these recurring thoughts. "Perhaps the blast of the bomb wouldn't even register in my ears. Would it take my legs off like it did my friend Tom?" This constant internal inquisition never ceased. "Would the bullet pass through me or would it hit a bone and start the death tumble within my body? What would the pain feel like? Would it be quick? Would my "Oppos" (Marine talk for friends) come to my rescue? Would I lie bleeding for long? Would the combat bandage stop the bleeding? Would I be able to stick the morphine needle into my leg?"

My mind relentlessly played out every imaginable scenario. What else was there to think about? Oh yes …"Watch out for possible sniper positions." It was like walking around with a noose around my neck. I felt like cannon fodder. At any given moment pain could sear my body. My thoughts became despondent. "Why don't you just get on with it, the stress of waiting is just too much." All the while, throughout the endless trauma of combat, my mind was developing deeper and hidden scar tissue. A baseline of sorts was established that set new barriers to keep me from living in the present. Little did I know what was being recorded in my mind. These past traumas would eventually displace present-day thoughts. The horror cloud of the past would encroach upon my ability to live in the moment, to have any semblance of peace.

During combat, my thoughts became increasingly negative—my stressed mind was preparing for the worst-case scenario. Even so I was simultaneously bombarded with thoughts of what to do in the case of a "Contact." What was the drill? Scream "Take cover," safety off, move, seek cover, instruct the lads what to do, report the situation on the radio, "Contact, wait out…." That waiting and wondering,

"Am I next?" Glancing over to where one Marine was on the ground...bleeding...screaming in pain. "Should that have been me? Is that what it looks like...not at all like the movies. Is that what I'll look like when it's my turn?" Witnessing the actual agony of a man shot, such horror.

Now more than thirty years later, a brilliant thought has just occurred to me. There has never been a report that the Loch Ness monster has eaten anyone! Why, old "Nessie" is most likely a vegetarian! That revelation has made me laugh out loud. I wonder, as an adult, if I still suffer the image of the boogieman under the bed? It is rather interesting to know that some monster-seeking people have installed cameras, waiting and watching 24/7 to capture a look at Nessie. Might there be a camera that could capture the "monster" in my mind? Thank God that He sent His Son to set the captives free.

In truth, all those returning from war are wounded in some manner. Going to war will leave a physical and/or an emotional scar; even a gaping wound. Some come home in a box. Some come home limping and missing a limb, an eye, or half a face. Some come home with a mind so traumatized; one wonders whether combat ever has a victor. "Welcome home, son!" Now what, God? How do I get on with my life? How will others view me? Will the stigma of an emotional war wound hound me for the rest of my life? How can I help my wife deal with me when my mind goes back to those horrible places? How can I cope with such a heavy burden? Can I keep all this hidden from others? How can I ever fit into society again after what I've seen? How can I be normal? What do others think of me? Am I being judged? Have you any idea what I went through? Is there anyone who will listen to me? Does anyone really care? How can anyone ever understand?

These are the words and thoughts that are shared with

me whenever I minister to those who are unpacking their hidden war wounds, their real or imaginary bandages as they are being unwound in prayer. During those times, I hear the words of our Lord demanding in John 11:43, *Lazarus come out!* It is as if Jesus Himself was shouting: "Come out of the wilderness. Come out of that cave. You are not dead. Come to Me, take off your bandages and live! You are set free, born again with new life in Me, free to live in all the abundance of the resurrection. Put all this behind you and live, really live!"

My prayer for you, who are bound by the bandages of past wounds, is for freedom. With bandages so tightly tied, living becomes extremely difficult. Removing them can free you to live life to the fullest, to have permission to come out of the cave of depression and despair and be freed to live again. Though the memories are not erased, they can be healed. When the bandages are removed, the healed you is revealed. Your past remains part of you, but the present becomes a continuation of your healing. It is sacred and holy. God will heal you in a way that only He can.

Not so long ago I led a group in a day long-retreat that focused on the healing of depression. A deeply sad man and his wife joined us. Though he had not read the Bible, he had been fixated for over thirty-five years on a single sentence…"Thou shall not kill." When I asked about his history, he told me that he was a Vietnam veteran and had killed many people. He said he was haunted by the words of Jesus…"Thou shall not kill." Together we looked at the Bible and I shared with him that a truer translation is: *You shall not commit murder.* Exodus 20:13 (Amplified Bible). Then I showed him another passage in the Bible and asked him to read it aloud to the rest of the group. Between loud sobs, he read from Ecclesiastes 3:1-3: *There is a time for everything…a time to kill and a time to heal."*

It was truly amazing as guilt and pain left this man in

but an instant. I shared with him how the late 1960s had been a time to kill or to be killed; but that *now* is the time to heal. This man's countenance changed before our very eyes, and his wife was smiling all the while. The dreadful torment and guilt that he had carried for three decades was lifted off his shoulders in an instant, in the blink of an eye. The healing love and compassion of Christ released him from dreadful self-condemning, emotional pain and reframed his life in the Truth that sets us free. God shined His Light on the monster of guilt and despair and set him free to live life to the fullest. Romans 8:1 says it all: *Therefore there is now no condemnation for those who are in Christ Jesus.*

It took many years before I was set free from the clutches of the monster that terrorized my own mind. Three years passed, after the traumas I sustained in combat, before I was pushed over the edge. My mind stopped dead and I imploded. It was not an explosion, it was an internal implosion. Much like a detonated bomb where air is violently pushed out and is thrust back with equal force, my whole mind and body imploded. I have seen the aftermath of a bomb's impact on shop windows, where glass took on an almost liquid parabolic curve as it drove inward and was followed by a terrifying implosion as the glass changed direction and flew back with dynamic force...shattering into thousands of projectiles flying in every direction. I witnessed it kill, maim, and scar people on its brutal mission. I recall my desperation as I hoped that it would not come anywhere near me.

What horror! What does one do with memories of people being sliced to shreds? I was so close to those bombs that when they exploded, I would remain deafened for several days. That monster overpowered me. It just had too much control.

I know that true power and glory comes from God,

who is still very much in the business of healing. Jesus is the same yesterday, today, and forever. Thank God! These memory monsters can be removed. They can positively be taken from your mind, tamed and returned to whence they came. The memories of the past, though not erased, can be sorted out and put in their right place. That place is where the memory monsters can no longer produce a troubling, involuntary physical response in the body of one suffering from post-traumatic stress disorder. When the DVD is played again, it can be rendered powerless over a tamed and healed mind. As healing continues, gone will be the days when every sinew is tensed in self-defense and when your tormented mind assumed a defensive stance as though the trauma was happening again, and again, and again.

Traumatic memories are like the frenzied activity of being on a hamster wheel, perpetual motion—yet going nowhere. Through Jesus Christ healing is purposeful and can calm the body and the mind. I am living proof that the monster can be tamed. Through God, I conquered PTSD. I am fully alive today; free indeed; no longer a slave to the painful memories of the past. You, also, can be set free!

CHAPTER TWO

A History of PTSD

*The guards were so afraid of him
that they shook and became like dead men.*
Matthew 28:4

On the morning of the resurrection which we now celebrate as Easter Sunday, two women, Mary Magdalene and "the other" Mary went to look at the tomb. An earthquake shook the earth violently. Then an angel appeared, rolled back the stone and in triumph, sat on it! The Bible describes the angel as being radiantly white with his appearance like lightning. It must have been both terrifying and exciting for the two Mary's to have witnessed that angel defiantly perched on death's door.

The local religious leaders and the Roman authorities were not going to be made fools of. Scripture tells us that they were very concerned that the followers of Jesus would steal His body and proclaim to all, "He is risen." I believe religious and military leaders would have chosen their top military guards to make sure that the theft of His body did not occur. I'm sure they chose the cream of the crop, the most reliable and seasoned soldiers they could find. But despite their best effort look what happened: *the guards were so afraid of the angel that they shook and became like dead men."* Matthew 28:4. I wonder if this is the first recorded case of acute stress that might have morphed into PTSD?

Looking back some fifteen hundred years prior to the resurrection, perhaps Moses also suffered trauma. The

13

rejection he may have felt, having been left as an infant in a floating basket by his mother, might have been a trauma that affected him for the rest of his life. Might Moses have been, in fact, the quintessential "basket case"?

But back to our resurrection narrative. We know that these crack guards were incapacitated by fear because we're told that they literally shook and then passed out! Having spent many hours on guard duty, I can relate. I most likely would have done the same! Now read this: *The angel said to the women, "Do not be afraid, for I know that you are looking for Jesus, who was crucified. He is not here; he has risen, just as he said. Come and see the place where he lay."* Matthew 28:5-6. Those crack guards had passed out, were rendered useless, incapacitated, like dead men; but the two women remained on their feet! This is one for the women! The angel told the women not to be afraid, but the men became as dead, incapacitated by fear. One name given to PTSD is "the thousand yard stare," becoming like a dead man as the mind closes down and locks in on the visual memory of past trauma. The mind tries to block out the present by repeatedly returning to the terror, the trauma, and the suffering of the past.

In my efforts to understand this disorder I have found that some of the names or aliases that have been given to PTSD over the years are very descriptive, almost poetic. The names give deeper insight into how the mind tries to cope with trauma. Some of these names liken PTSD to fragmentation, much like a hand grenade as it explodes. In my ministry of healing, I see the scattering and dissociation of thoughts and coping skills in the diagnosis of Dissociative Identity Disorder (DID), an extreme form of PTSD often caused by satanic ritual abuse (SRA). The various names given to this malady in the past, were almost kindly in their descriptiveness, whereas "PTSD" sounds so clinical, antiseptic or business-like. A proper diagnosis, however, is critical for medical insurance purposes. The fourth edition of the Diagnostic and Statistical Manual of Mental Disorders (DSM-IV) is the manual used in the USA, to provide common language, a base line or standard for all who treat PTSD, to use in completing insurance claims. Officially naming this condition "Post Traumatic Stress Disorder" has provided the clinical sound that it very much needs today.

As we survey the names given to this malady in the past, it is important to note that PTSD is not new. This is not just happening to you. You are not alone. For thousands of years, people have suffered this disorder. Over the history of man, victims have tried to cope with PTSD and make sense of their shattered lives. Sadly, it would seem that in the present time, our lives and brains are being subjected to ever more horrifying trauma. When our lives are threatened, whether this is real or perceived, we become vulnerable to this condition.

In chronological order, let's look at some of the names formerly given to this condition now called PTSD:

Ancient Greeks

Long ago in ancient Greece—mothers, wives, and girlfriends noticed a difference in their men when they returned from war. Though there is no record of a name being given to what they observed, it is reported that men returning from combat were deemed "different." Just think on that, this dates all the way back to the ancient Greeks! Ancient Greece is known as belonging to the period of history lasting hundreds of years from the archaic period (800-600 B.C.) up to 146 BC when the Romans defeated the Greeks at the Battle of Corinth. That was 2,156 years ago! This condition is NOT new.

Nostalgia

In the 1700s during the Revolutionary War of America's fight for independence, when returning soldiers behaved in an unfamiliar way they were regarded as suffering "nostalgia." These men seemed to have been changed by their battlefield experiences. Those suffering "nostalgia" just sat there, vacant, seemingly lost in their thoughts of the past. Later named the "thousand yard stare" in the Vietnam era.

Railway Spine

During the Victorian era in the United Kingdom (circa 1837-1901), the name "railway spine" was given to PTSD. The origin of this name fascinates me. In the early days of train travel there were many accidents when trains either derailed or collided with one another. Passengers traveling aboard those trains that wrecked were subjected to a condition we now call "whiplash." Physicians at that time thought that the physical injury of whiplash caused a mental disorder. The British mindset of "a stiff upper lip" may have contributed to the view that physical injury was responsible for subsequent mental problems among traumatized surviving passengers. Doctors did not connect the mental anguish of the survivors with their having witnessed the horrible carnage of mangled steel and human bodies. Of course we know better today, but, at that time, survivor's guilt and traumatic memories were not linked to their lingering mental problems.

Irritable Heart

An "irritable heart" was one of the names given to those soldiers suffering from PTSD during World War I. This name accurately describes the condition and the effects of trauma upon the minds and bodies of those who were engaged in combat. Incredible irritability is just one of the presenting symptoms associated with post trauma today.

Soldier's Heart

Another name ascribed to those traumatized by combat during WWI is "soldier's heart." This name is kindly in its characterization of the condition we know today as PTSD which afflicted returning soldiers. I personally like this descriptive name because it addresses the wounded heart, the seat of emotion of those who have been emotionally damaged in combat.

Neurasthenia

Neurasthenia is a psycho-pathological term first used by George Miller Beard in 1869 to denote a condition with symptoms of fatigue, anxiety, headache, neuralgia, and depressed mood. Though it is currently a diagnosis in the World Health Organization's International Classification of Diseases, it is no longer included as a diagnosis in the American Psychiatric Association's Diagnostic and Statistical Manual of Mental Disorders. During World War I, however, neurasthenia was a common diagnosis.

Shell Shock

Yet another name first given to PTSD victims in WWI and perpetuated in WWII was a condition known as "shell shock." To be honest, it is my favorite name, as it really describes the mind's reaction to war and to the sudden onslaught of noise, terror, and fear. This is the diagnosis I was given in 1978.

Post-Vietnam Syndrome

This whole problem of post-war issues really came to the forefront during the Vietnam conflict. Not only did those chaps suffer in hand to hand combat, but then they came home to a barrage of constant insult which grew out of years of political unrest and civilian protests against the war. Expecting a hero's welcome, Vietnam-era soldiers returned home to yet another war of sorts as they were spat upon and cursed. Sadly, these painful memories are still very much alive in the minds of many Vietnam veterans today. These veterans were not welcomed back in any manner comparable to what combatants receive today. Instead they were called "baby killers," and more pain was heaped upon their wounded minds. Vietnam veterans were re-traumatized with every hostility hurled at them by those who spewed anti-war sentiments and who held them accountable for the war itself.

The Thousand Yard Stare

An expression of PTSD widely observed in Vietnam vets occurs when a victim cannot function or respond, even when triggered, named "the thousand yard stare" because those suffering just totally shut down and vacantly stare off at some distant point. The horrific battle going on in their minds closes off any communication. It's as though a fuse has been blown. They appear expressionless as though they are dead. The internal turmoil is so great that their brains cannot function; they just shut down in total overload. In the late 1970s this happened to me many times. At those times my brain put me back there, right in the middle of the "contact," as I relived the trauma over and over again. It was all internal, an internal violence that, quite frankly, created a frightening and terrible battle for sanity. It was very difficult for me to come out of those episodes on my own. When I could not, I was injected to help me fall asleep quickly. I have no idea how it affected others around me. Now, over thirty years later, I shudder as I recall those episodes. I thank God that I have been healed of this traumatized response to the replaying of those images in my mind. When I am privileged to pray for others who are still suffering these reactions, I often pray for God to rewire their damaged brains. You will read more on this topic later, particularly in a discussion of the healing of memories.

War Neurosis

A more graphic name for PTSD is "war neurosis." The name speaks for itself: the phobia, the fixation, the psychosis, the obsession, the horror of what one has seen and experienced. I met a policeman suffering from PTSD who was showing signs of neurosis as he dealt with the aftermath of a car crash. A beautiful girl with whom he had attended high school had been killed in that crash. He had always liked her. At the scene it was his job to pick up her decapitated head, by her blond hair, so she could be placed in a body bag. This poor chap was devastated with horror and sadness. As he shared his story, his right hand shook while his left hand made motions of washing the memory away. He was so traumatized by what he had experienced that his actions did not surprise me at all. Listening to him, I was personally shaken, as were about twenty-five other first responders also present. There wasn't a dry eye in the room. The outpouring of love for this chap from all those present was amazing. There is always potential for suffering compassion fatigue even by those who simply listen as trauma is recounted. Such stories affect us to our cores. I hadn't thought about this particular story for years. Reading over this now and remembering how I felt as I listened to him has actually evoked a physical response within me. I feel ill. I need to go and pray for my own memory of this and once again be filled with Christ's peace.

Battle Fatigue

"Battle fatigue" is perhaps the best known name given to post-trauma suffering. The raw fear, the experience of things seen and unseen, eating away at the mind, results in an emotional cancer. Victims say they are just "sick and tired of being sick and tired." Or they state, "This is all just too much." Or they question, "How can I go out on yet another patrol?" Or the woman who was attacked may wonder to herself, "How can I park my car again in the parking lot where I was raped?" A constant incoming of memories can be triggered by something on TV, by a car backfiring, by a word from a friend, or from situations that cause the DVD to replay that same footage over and over again, ad nauseam. It is all-consuming and utterly exhausting.

Compassion Fatigue

Another name for PTSD is "compassion fatigue," which can impact both the victim of trauma and the one who cares for the victim. Do individuals have a maximum capacity for absorbing trauma? Does a caregiver reach a limit when the "enough already" button gets pushed? Can the war veteran, the victim of abuse, or the caregiver reach a point of overload? Of these three, the caregiver is perhaps the most likely to be affected by compassion fatigue. Listening to their stories, over and over again, I have heard the cry of caregivers who became saturated with the trauma of those for whom they are tasked to care. Can a person helping another reach an end point where caring becomes too much for their soul?

It's complicated, but yes. Yes—because when overload is reached, it is likely that we have voluntarily exceeded what is necessary in caring for another. In 1 Corinthians 10:13 you will find, *The temptations in your life are no different from what others experience. And God is faithful. He will not allow the temptation to be more than you can stand. When you are tempted, he will show you a way out so that you can endure.* In this passage we learn that the Lord does not require more of us than we can handle, but when we feel overloaded, He will provide a way for us to endure.

About a year after the 9/11 tragedy, I had the opportunity to learn more about compassion fatigue when I was asked to assist many therapists from New York and it's environs who were seeking prayer. For nearly a year they had heard the same horrific stories recounted over and over again and were now suffering from compassion fatigue. They were, themselves, traumatized. They needed prayer to help them cope individually with the onslaught of an overwhelming corporate need for healing and resolution. It had become a massive problem for them as they experienced a never-ending rush of immense pain, exacerbated by seemingly endless television coverage and images of planes striking the twin towers. The entire nation became repeatedly traumatized, as were the therapists, counselors, and clergy whom the public depended upon for help.

Caring for others day after day can be extremely draining. We all need a place to recharge our batteries, either an actual physical location or a restful place in our minds. We need to go to that place and recover, for our own sake and for the sake of those needing our care. Being alone somewhere, visiting a favorite pond or a park, going to a movie, or having coffee with a friend, can help restore serenity and rest to our souls. It is helpful to know that our need to get away, to carve out time for ourselves, is normal, natural, and necessary.

Some caregivers feel very guilty when leaving their charges in order to "recharge" themselves. Though they may take a morning off, they may spend all their time away feeling dreadful. Such false guilt can eat away at their souls.

The sheer volume of work and nurture provided by caregivers inevitably results in this condition known as "compassion fatigue." Though it is totally understandable and a natural outgrowth of the demands placed on caregivers, it is not often discussed. Compassion fatigue sufferers may begin to have troubling thoughts assail their minds such as, "Hurry up and die, so I can get on with my life," as the trauma of guilt and dread assaults their emotions, compounding their already exhausted and vulnerable bodies and minds. Many people when going through divorce have told me confidentially, "If only my spouse's brakes would fail, then I can get this all behind me and get on with my life." Unspoken, mounting guilt exhausts the caregiver *and* the post-trauma victim. Let me say this again: these feelings are quite natural but need to be addressed. Those feeling such conflict should seek help and "get permission" to take leave to have some personal recharging. If your house isn't clean, how can you clean someone else's?

My purpose in writing this section is to help you recognize the signs and possible existence of this condition. Sufferers of compassion fatigue have overloaded their minds and souls, and they are constantly struggling. We have to maintain a balance between work, prayer, time off, exercise, relaxation, and hobbies. We all need some time that allows us to get lost in something that really fascinates us. This balance is achieved by taking "self-time," when we can lose hours and have no need to look at a clock! It can also be of immense help to have a spiritual director, someone to talk to and to unload your mental frustrations. Friends are only good to a point; sometimes we need objective counsel. The key here, again, is balance. Maintaining balance in life is vitally important to being set free from compassion fatigue.

PTS

Recently, the U.S. Army has evolved the name even further. They have dropped the term 'disorder,' and now simply categorize it 'Post-Traumatic Stress.' In doing so, they are suggesting that PTS is a normative reaction to combat without signifying an attached nomenclature burden.

In Summary

Having examined the many names given for PTSD, it is obvious that whatever name it goes by, PTSD hurts immensely. Most people do not understand the sufferer, much less what the sufferer has suffered. The strange thing about this disorder is that if a group of people are subjected to the identical trauma, say a hijacking, not all of the people involved will develop PTSD symptoms. A military section of soldiers may come under fire, but not all will react later in the same way. This raises many questions about what is in the mind. Why are some people affected while others are symptom free? What pushes some into the darkest storm of the mind while others remain in safe harbor?

Regardless of the answers to those questions, we have the Good News. Jesus came to set the captives free. We can read in Luke 4:16-18 the spoken words of Jesus that were first written by the prophet Isaiah 61:1-2, approximately 700 years before Jesus' birth: *Jesus went to Nazareth, where he had been brought up, and on the Sabbath day he went into the synagogue, as was his custom. And he stood up to read. The scroll of the prophet Isaiah was handed to him. Unrolling it, he found the place where it is written: "The Spirit of the Lord is on me, because he has anointed me to preach good news to the poor. He has sent me to proclaim freedom for the prisoners and recovery of sight for the blind, to release the oppressed, to proclaim the year of the Lord's favor."* Jesus came to give freedom to prisoners, those imprisoned in their minds by what they have seen and experienced. He is still releasing those who are oppressed. The oppression of past trauma is released as the memory of it is healed.

Some while ago at The Falls Church in Virginia, I was leading a healing mission which went from Friday night through Saturday, ending with a healing service on Sunday. As I taught about healing on Saturday, I focused on setting the captives free and unpacked the above Bible verses. The altar rail sections had been removed just for the day in order to create open space. As I spoke of setting the captives free, the Spirit of the Sovereign Lord came upon me. I was suddenly given a revelation. I felt led to one section of the altar rail that had been set aside. I picked it up and held it before my face. It was very heavy and I could not hold it for long. Then God gave me the picture of what it was like for me to be captive to PTSD. As I held up that rail, I saw that I was imprisoned. The vertical rails looked like a wall of a prison cell. God's revelation was, that... yes, I am imprisoned, but there is only one wall to that cell! I was holding on to it for dear life because it was so heavy. I was owning it. It was *my* cell, *my* prison, *my* pain. The realization that there was only one wall hit me like a freight train. My focus had been on that single wall. Looking out from my imaginary cell, through this one wall, I glanced to my left and to my right and then behind me. To my shock, there were no other walls! I now put this very heavy section of altar rail down in front of me and walked away from that prison cell. I realized that I was not in prison at all. The three other walls were not there! I had lived in the prison of my mind, a prison that was missing three walls. I was now free indeed. The Lord had set me free!

So, dear friend, what prison walls have you erected around yourself? What prison walls have been put up by others? How many walls are there around you? Look to your left and to your right and realize, as I did, that you are free. Let go of the pain and wounds. Walk away with Christ's help. Please understand that this is just the start of your healing, but it *is* the start. I hope this visual image will help you begin your healing journey. I will go into more depth about the process of inner healing and the healing of memories in future chapters of this book.

CHAPTER THREE

Near Death Experiences
of the Body and Mind

Hezekiah's Illness

In those days Hezekiah became ill and was at the point of death. The prophet Isaiah son of Amoz went to him and said, "This is what the LORD says: Put your house in order, because you are going to die; you will not recover." Hezekiah turned his face to the wall and prayed to the LORD, "Remember, O LORD, how I have walked before you faithfully and with wholehearted devotion and have done what is good in your eyes." And Hezekiah wept bitterly. Before Isaiah had left the middle court, the word of the LORD came to him: "Go back and tell Hezekiah, the leader of my people, 'This is what the LORD, the God of your father David, says: I have heard your prayer and seen your tears; I will heal you. On the third day from now you will go up to the temple of the LORD. I will add fifteen years to your life."

2 Kings 20:1-6

King Hezekiah was told that he was going to die. He was told to get his life in order in preparation for his death. He prayed, bargaining with God, *Remember, O LORD, how I have walked before you faithfully and with wholehearted devotion and have done what is good in your eyes.* God heard Hezekiah's prayer. He saw his tears and healed him. Hezekiah was given life, fifteen more years of life. I feel a bit like this king. For some strange reason I have had at least a dozen close shaves with death. Some of them were closer than others, but He has kept me around a little longer; hopefully a lot longer than fifteen years!

My earliest close shaves with death were during combat in the early 1970s. I was shot at three times and had all but forgotten about the *whiz*, that familiar stinging buzzing sound of the rounds, until I saw the movie "Saving Private Ryan." I wanted to run out of that movie theatre. The movie brought back memories of three separate occasions on patrol when rounds just missed me. I heard the bullets. I knew where they were in relation to my body but I couldn't see them. One shot went by my head on the left side, another on my right at about shoulder height, and still another passed by my left hip. It was not till later, after the "contact" report was sent, that my mind registered what had happened. As I absorbed the danger I had been in, I privately shook and felt enormous relief that those rounds had missed me. It was terrifying, such an insult to my mind and body. But I didn't really feel its impact until later.

As I write this I am back there once again hearing the sounds with heightened awareness, ever vigilant. My blood pressure is up right now and I can feel butterflies in my stomach as I recall this in vivid detail. I remember a friend with whom I had joined the Marines. He was very tall, perhaps too tall, as he died when one of those buzzing rounds hit him in the head. Though I was madder than heck and wanted to shoot back at the enemy, I'm grateful that I was never in a position to return fire; one less thing I've had to reckon with. I realize as I write this now, that I had never thought this through before. So many soldiers have recounted their vivid memories to me, sharing what they recorded when they pulled the trigger, especially snipers who saw the result of their actions in full telescopic view. Such memories are imprinted, input through the eye and replayed like a slide show or streaming DVD in the mind.

At five different times in combat, I nearly lost my life

to exploding bombs. It was terrifying not to know where a bomb might be hidden. Perhaps there's one in a box? In a car? In some random package in the mail? Each time the scenario was the same: relative calm was suddenly shattered by the shock of the explosion. My head felt crushed by the deafening noise. My whole body felt impacted by a brutal punch. My eyes ached. Even the hair on my head hurt! Often brain damage results from the violent impact of a bomb. During the worst explosion that I survived, the severity of the blast literally picked me up and threw me, bodily, into a door. It felt like a full body kick or a severe punch to my chest and groin. I remember checking myself off, I inventoried myself…counted my fingers, checked for blood in my ears, and so on.

One of the most horrific bomb explosions I experienced occurred at a chocolate factory, of all places. The calm was once again broken by the shock of the explosion and then the sound of screams. Most of the victims were slashed violently by flying glass. It was all quite sickening as we hurriedly bandaged the victims in an effort to curtail the loss of blood. I was fortunate to have survived this one, but some of my buddies died there or died later of the mortal wounds they had sustained. To this day I am not fond of the smell of chocolate.

A bomb blast that occurred in a shopping district devastated me as my mind struggled to work out the resulting carnage I witnessed that day. I distinctly remember a fire alarm bell that would just not stop ringing. To this day, the sound of a fire alarm distresses me. A BBC camera crew arrived on the scene and filmed the mayhem. The next day I called home and my parents told me that they had seen me on television during the nine o'clock news and were traumatized as they watched. It took me much longer to recognize how deep my own trauma was from it. All of these memories festered in my mind over time, resulting in an emotional cancer that provided more fodder for PTSD. Looking back on it now, I see the cumulative impact of these traumas as a sort of fungus that mushroomed out of control and infected my right mind. At that time Critical Incident Debriefing (CID) had not yet been implemented. The use of CID today, can help combat personnel to process their thoughts and feelings and promote healing. But back then, we just did the British "stiff-upper-lip" thing, had a cup of tea and got on with the job at hand.

When I was a young Royal Marine, I nearly drowned on the island of Malta in the Mediterranean. It was a Sunday morning, and though all eight of us had hangovers, we rented scuba diving gear. The stupidity of youth! I had never been diving before and did not know that my weight belt was too heavy for my size. We did a sort of test drive near the Blue Grotto by dipping down from a standing position to test our masks and any other problems with our gear. We then swam down an underwater valley out of the small bay, at about seventy feet below surface. I sat on the bottom sand with rocks on either side of me and when I looked up there was water in my mask. Though I had been paired up with another Marine, I didn't know where he was. The water in my mask began to choke me and I had no idea how to clear my mask. Sheer panic set in as water went up my nose. I did precisely what you are not supposed to do: I shot up as fast as I could and broke the surface, gasping in a quick lung full of fresh air. But my weight belt pulled me back down into the deep. I then realized that, in my panic, I'd not only lost my flippers and mask, but I couldn't find my regulator or mouth piece either!

I held my breath and pushed up to take another breath, and then did the drowning-man swim to the shore. The shoreline was too steep and the rocks were very jagged.

I could not get out. I shouted for help, but no one came. Weakened and unable to stay afloat, I sank back underwater and could no longer hold my breath. I thought, "I'm going to die. Is this how I'm going to die?" My lungs were bursting and I had to take a breath ... of water! I saw a flashing movie of my life. I was in sheer panic, but as the water filled my lungs, a deep peace came upon me. I had a vision of a yellow tube going to heaven; not straight up, but rising over the horizon. The tube was just wide enough for my shoulders. It was so beautiful, so peaceful. It was as if I was being drawn up into this umbilical cord to heaven. It was so amazing. But I don't know what happened next. Everything just went blank.

When I came to, I was pushing myself up on the back seat of a moving car, vomiting water all over the place. It was then that I saw a bus heading straight at us and realized that our car was traveling on the wrong side of the road. A friend was driving like a madman to get me to the hospital. I passed out again, thinking that I might possibly die in a head-on collision.

The next time I gained consciousness, I heard the familiar sound of helicopter rotors. I found myself on a gurney next to a chopper as a medic assessed whether I needed time in a hyperbaric chamber to recover from the bends. Without knowing the details, it was assumed that I had surfaced too rapidly and needed oxygen to recover. Finally I heard the helicopter lift off without me. I spent the next three days in the hospital bandaged from head to toe, having been badly cut up by those rocks on the shoreline. My buddies nicknamed me, "Mummy Mumford." I found out later that a Royal Navy diver had heard my cry for help and had pulled me out. He resuscitated me. I never met that chap, nor have I learned his name; but if he is reading this account now: I want to thank you for saving my life and may God bless you!

Of course there was the time I nearly died in a helicopter piloted by none other than His Royal Highness Prince Charles! We were having major problems trying to land at sea on the carrier, as it was pitching and yawing. When Prince Charles tried to set our orange helo down, just one tire hit the deck. As a result, the helo bounced back to the other wheel and then pitched back again. This time the rotor blades hit the deck and we watched in horror as the deck crew ran for their lives. Then came the red light and the emergency klaxon alarm sounded inside the helo. We just sat there bouncing around waiting to die. Then somehow in the next moment, the orange bird regained flight and after flying around a bit in preparation, Prince Charles executed a perfect landing.

In another close shave I nearly died, along with three thousand others, when the ship I was aboard almost collided with a Russian spy ship in the Mediterranean Sea. The Russians had been taking photos of us refueling at sea. Fortunately we all escaped harm. I am reminded of these near misses as there were so very many. In my first book, *Hand to Hand: From Combat to Healing*, I recounted in greater detail an episode where a man pointed a machine gun at me and another Marine. It became a standoff in an alley. Each and every time, death came close but did not take me.

So why am I telling you these stories? I'm setting the stage for sharing the trauma that would ultimately cripple my mind. The accumulated trauma associated with all these near death experiences continued to build up within me, until I was finally pushed over the edge. That's when my mind just shut down as I fell into the clutches of Post-Traumatic Stress Disorder.

Flash Back

Flash backs, or abreactions, are often experienced by victims of trauma. They occur when an incident is replayed in the mind and the body reacts by releasing huge amounts of adrenalin. The victim is carried by the adrenalin rush into a fight-flight alert to stay alive. I had totally forgotten about the following incident until the Fourth of July this year. The flash and bangs of fireworks had instantly brought me back to my training before going to combat. I hadn't thought of this event since the day it happened in 1973. This memory took thirty-seven years to surface! It was another near-death experience that I'd pushed away, a new memory I had never dealt with.

Seeing the flashes and hearing the bangs of the fireworks reminded me of the colorful words of our Sergeant Major when he exploded in pure rage, one day, at the grenade range. We were trained to clean out grenades of wax and grease, then prime them with fuses. The fuses are not to be touched because the heat from your fingers can set them off. On this occasion, I had cleaned three grenades, set their pins, and put them on my belt, ready to be thrown. I assumed the stance, put my right forefinger in the ring, pulled the pin, put my right hand up, and checked that the pin was in the ring. I then stretched out my left hand, looked for the target, and threw it with all my might. I started to count. I watched it land, per protocol, and then hit the deck fast. "Five, six, seven." Nothing. It was supposed to go off after seven seconds! No explosion. Silence!

The grenade had not gone off, but the Sergeant Major did. He exploded. Quietly at first, then gradually growing louder and louder until he reached full volume fury. He accused me of not cleaning the weapon properly. He glared at me with raw anger. Suddenly he bellowed, "Okay men,

I will now teach you how to deal with an unexploded ordinance!" He instructed the rest of the troop to stay in the throwing bunker and keep their heads down while he and I approached the unexploded bomb with two more grenades, a fuse, and some plastic explosive (PE). I was shaking like a leaf! He had me stand about three feet from the unexploded grenade as he calmly told me that the spring could release at any moment and that the two of us would not even hear it go off. How reassuring was that! It did nothing to help my shakes.

The Sergeant Major then very carefully molded the PE around the two extra grenades and inserted the fuse into the explosive. He then placed the two extra grenades on either side of the lame one. Then he told me to light the fuse…twenty seconds worth of time until lift off! Still shaking considerably, I lit the fuse. We then had to walk away as you're less likely to fall if you walk, rather than run. It was the longest walk I have ever taken. ("Dead man walking" comes to mind now!) All the while he was still cursing me. We both were counting as we ducked down behind the protective wall. "Eighteen, nineteen, twenty." BOOM! Wow, it was impressive. Three hand grenades and a quarter pound of PE made the Fourth of July fireworks pale in comparison. I then got a serious dressing down from the Sergeant Major. When the rest of the troop resumed throwing more grenades, we found four more defective grenades from that same box. Four more lads had to walk out with the Sergeant Major and carry out the same drill I had earlier. It took a while until he decided that we were not to throw any more grenades from that box! The only vindication I received after being falsely accused was that he obliged me with a grunt.

What's my point here? A hand grenade is a double-sided weapon; it can kill the person who throws it just as it can kill the person at whom it is thrown! The plug of a grenade does the most damage as the rest of the thing breaks up! It is designed to wound, not kill. A wounded man takes several more people and resources away from the battle as they try to help him. Sadly, no one helps a dead man in the midst of combat, except perhaps a chaplain.

Have you ever thrown a grenade? Did you ever consider that you need not be in combat to throw out just as deadly an ordinance as a primed grenade? What we speak can wound just as aggressively and even be terminal. So when you throw out something negative, it is much like a grenade in its ability to be double-sided. What we say with our tongues can hurt us, as well as those who hear us. We can throw physical hand grenades, and we can throw out verbal grenades; both do serious damage.

My most recent brush with death happened in October of 2009. The H1N1 virus (swine flu) hit me so hard it nearly ended my life. I'll share more of that story later in this book. Though I've had many close calls, when I got to number nine I thought to myself, "If I were a cat, I would be very nervous now!" Well I am obviously not a cat, as I have now survived many more than nine. Thanks be to God! I stand on the promise of God:

I have heard your prayer and seen your tears; I will heal you. 2 Kings 20:5

CHAPTER FOUR

The War Abroad: An Unseen Invasion of the Mind

And there was war in heaven. Michael and his angels fought against the dragon, and the dragon and his angels fought back.

Revelation 12:7

My husband is not at home; he has gone on a long journey.

Proverbs 7:19

The thing that finally pushed me over the edge was the "dragon" in my mind, like the one referenced in Revelation 12:7, my dragon kept fighting back within me. I suffered what is known as "shell shock," the result of the many combat traumas I had endured. I now see, with 20/20 hindsight, that these were an accumulation of "stressors." Most of them involved witnessing people die during combat, forcing me to reckon with my own imminent death. I experienced a steady buildup of such traumas, each one heaped onto the others, like Lego blocks piled so high that just one more topples the entire stack. I was like a pressure cooker. It was far too much for my brain to handle. Wasn't I supposed to be a tough Royal Marine Commando Green Beret drill instructor? What has happened to me?

Three years after my last active combat duty, I was serving as a drill instructor at the Commando Training School when I heard about four soldiers, fresh from basic training, who had died of a bomb blast while on patrol. It was this particular Lego block that toppled my stack and shoved me into the despair of PTSD. The shocking news of their death played right into my deep-seated fear that one day Marines, I had trained, would die in combat. For many years I believed, without any real proof, that I had been the drill instructor who had taken those four lads through their basic training. I do not know how I came to suppose that, but that is what I believed. Looking back on this now, I recognize that my mind was really not too healthy and that the news of their deaths was the last straw. In my seared psyche, the thing I had feared the most had happened. *What I feared has come upon me; what I dreaded has happened to me. I have no peace, no quietness; I have no rest, but only turmoil.* Job 3:25-26

Recently I did some research and found a book that reported all the deaths in that theater of war. I could not find the names of any of my recruits! I had been wrong! For so very long, my mind was certain of my responsibility in the death of four Marines. I was so convinced that I actually wrote of this event, as fact, in my book, *Hand to Hand: From Combat to Healing.* Shockingly, the dragon in my mind had managed to make me accept as true this utterly false information. I now know what really happened. Four chaps did die, and all were fresh recruits right from training, but they were from an Army unit. They were not Marines! I could not have trained them. I have since met their commanding officer, now retired, and was able to put all of this right in my mind. I felt such compassion for my brother soldier who was suffering the same grief as I had for all these years. Both of us blamed ourselves and had taken responsibility for their deaths. Sadly, our guilt served to do nothing more than torture our minds and keep us chained to our pain.

As a drill instructor my biggest fear was that those recruits trained by me would die in battle because I had not done a good enough job! I now know that this was erroneous thinking but, back then, as I tried to grasp the news of their deaths, I just totally shut down. I felt as though the bomb that killed them had detonated inside of me as well. I could not function. I could not speak. No sound came out of my mouth for one week. I was destroyed. (Later when I finally started to speak again, I had a very bad stutter for six months.) A doctor injected me with something to calm me down and I fell asleep. But when I returned to duty, I was not right. I have a recollection of my trip back, later that day, to the Commando Training School and stopping for gasoline. Still unable to speak, I tried to ask the attendant to "fill her up please." The words would just not come out of my mouth. The gas station attendant laughed at me and I felt my hand clench. Not a good situation. For a fleeting moment I wanted to respond the Marine way and fight back. I did stop myself from hitting him and, with a weak smile, gestured for him to fill the car with gas. In retrospect, I am so very grateful that I didn't do what I really wanted to do to that attendant. Somehow I had managed to keep my frustration in check.

So there I was—a drill instructor who could not speak. It was my job to communicate. But I was silenced. I arrived at the Commando Training School and avoided everyone that night. I reported to the troop officer in the morning who looked at me and gently told me to get myself to sickbay. I remember that walk of shame to sickbay as I circumnavigated the sacred parade ground. I was then taken by a Marine driver to Stonehouse Naval Hospital, Plymouth, Devon, where I was observed for three weeks. Ironically it was the same hospital where my father had spent six months recovering from a very nasty motorcycle accident while serving in the Navy.

The next six months were an utterly confusing hell on earth as I was slowly brought back to life. My mind was in total turmoil. I had no idea what was going on in my head. The dragon had a firm grip on me. I had never heard of "shell shock" before. At the time, I never asked questions to help me understand what was happening to me. Not once did I ask. I was in such a mess. The world as I knew it had shattered, and I had come unraveled. Nothing made sense.

I was dismissed from the Royal Marines, was given an honorable discharge and found myself driving to my parents' home. I was a very lost and confused soul. "What now, God?" Before I left, my commanding officer at the Commando Training School casually informed me, "this sort of thing happens a lot" and then went on to tell me not to worry about it! He even asked me if I'd like to continue in the Marines as a signaler. I looked at him blankly. "A –a-a-a signaler?" I stammered, "What-t-t-t does a signaler do?" The Lieutenant Colonel replied, "He communicates." I couldn't even talk properly! I stuttered so badly that it took ages for others to understand me. My astonished look and lack of response must have registered with him. He seemed slowly to grasp that I needed to get out of the business of teaching recruits to kill or be killed. I left the Marines broken, depressed, unemployed, and unemployable. What was I to do?

Upon returning home, my reactions to stress continued to escalate until I soon realized that I could not function in a right mind. Within a few short days I found myself in a civilian hospital. Any loud noise, or anything that startled me, closed me down. The hospital's weekly fire drills with their blaring fire alarm would send my mind into orbit. The fire alarm was my worst and fiercest trigger. It would shut me down and put me in a terrible place. Instantly memories of those chaps dying in that dreadful bombing would storm my conscious mind. Even today I have to really focus on the present moment when an alarm bell goes off. I am forever grateful to the less invasive digital noise of modern alarm clocks! I do so much better with them!

So where was God in all of this? Well I know that He was with me, but I was not with Him. I was a lost, broken and hurting man. Any external stimulus could trigger my agitated mind to jump into a flight-fight response mode. But, in reality, I could neither fight nor run away. What was there to fight? So instead I would zone out, just totally close down. This was a very nasty time in my life. It was the dark night of my soul, my tortured soul; condemned by overexposure to the threat of death, real and perceived. Jose Narosky has written, "In war, there are no unwounded soldiers." How true. My physical being was impacted by bombs exploding near me, causing internal damage to my brain. But my mind was equally damaged by what I had continually seen and recorded during combat.

Whenever I was abreacting, four men in white hospital coats would come and stick a needle in my rear. Minutes later I would fall fast asleep. That seemed to help, in that it defused the internal bomb. I met with a therapist every day. Bit by bit we unpacked the nasty dragon and my memories were processed. I also had several visits from clergy, but they weren't helpful with this trauma. They did, however, bring God to me very quietly. There were a few clergy who also suggested that I needed deliverance. I even wondered myself whether that could be true. The stigma of this disease resulted in guarded behavior toward others on my part, as well as guarded behavior by others toward me. Those treating me did not allow my friends to visit me because, in my state of mind, I might upset them or they might upset me. My heart still hurts that my closest friends were not allowed to visit. I now know that they were following doctors' orders, but, at the time, I felt like I had "mental leprosy." I suffered more rejection—real and perceived. Not one friend visited me the entire six months I remained there. Pain heaped upon more pain. Worse yet, it was not until the last week of my hospital stay that I was told what was wrong with me! It was not a form of demonic oppression, it was PTSD! What a relief it was finally to have a diagnosis and to be told that my behavior and reactions were entirely normal for someone who had experienced ongoing combat trauma.

The interior and invisible scars of combat had infected my mind. I met other patients in the civilian hospital who were also traumatized, just not from combat. One woman was a wounded soul on the inside because of what had happened to her on the outside. I could relate to her pain which was caused by her external scar. Looking at my new friend from her right profile, she was a pretty young woman. But when she turned her head to the left side, her physical wound was visible. She had been kicked in the face by a horse. The left side of her face was crumpled in. The scar on her face was the outline and shape of a horseshoe. While in the hospital, not having had reconstructive surgery yet, and she shared her very real fear of how people reacted to her appearance. Upon sight of her face, children drew back from her in fear and horror. Some people had even said very nasty things. My heart wept for her. As I considered her pain, I realized that her external scar touched my own internal and unseen scars. Her wound was visible, but I could totally understand what she was going through. She was as shattered and broken as I was. I've had no further contact with her since my hospitalization, but I pray that she has by now received the gift of a reconstructed face and is enjoying life.

I suspect that people can "see" the wounds of PTSD

just by looking at the symptoms of those who suffer with it. Though the wound of PTSD is invisible to the eye, it becomes as visible and prominent as a facial scar when others witness the behavior of those who suffer from it. The internal wound of PTSD is exposed and made "visible" to others when those who suffer with it are triggered and cannot control their reactions. Having PTSD is like being bandaged all around your head for a wound that cannot be seen and is not visibly bleeding. When the healing balm of prayer and therapy is applied to those unseen wounds of PTSD, the bandages can be removed, and a radiantly healed, unscarred "face" is revealed. If you feel that you are bandaged around your head for unseen wounds in your life, perhaps, with God's help, it's time to have the bandage removed. With PTSD your bandage is so tightly wrapped around your brain that it causes distortion. As you remove the bandage you can be freed from that "grave cloth," just as Lazarus was raised from the dead when Jesus called him forth from the tomb. Your suffering mind can be resurrected from PTSD and given new life!

As I write this book and dredge up these painful memories of my past, it has once again put me on edge. This is all stuff I have tried to hide from, tried not to talk about, tried to bury and give it a funeral of sorts. But this is who I am. I am a man healed of trauma, a man brought back from the brink of death on several occasions. I am a man severely traumatized who had a medical diagnosis of "shell shock." Yet I am a man who is ninety-nine percent healed. There is a little left that still has power over me, but not much! I've been healed by therapy and by God. I am a fully functioning member of society. As my mother very wisely said, "Nigel, God has recycled you." How true her words are. The recycling has allowed me to minister to first responders, even those grieving family members and therapists after 9/11. I am privileged now to minister to members of the armed forces suffering trauma in all wars from WWII to the present.

The dragon has been slain. I am free to live my life to the fullest, with abundant joy in and through the Lord. Jesus Christ is still very much in the healing business. There is now peace in my mind where the memories of war once had absolute power over me. Jesus came to set the captives free. I have been set free from all those horrendous memories and I am now able to live again!

CHAPTER FIVE

The War at Home: Domestic Abuse

If a man has recently married,
He must not be sent to war or have any
other duty laid on him.
For one year he is to be free to stay at home
And bring happiness to the wife he has married.

Deuteronomy 24:5

Sadly, the wisdom of this verse from Deuteronomy has been all but forgotten and is not practiced today. The stress of war threatens marital happiness, but so does daily life in general. Tensions build, bringing trauma into the would-be safety of the home, thus making war within the household. The sins of the father and indeed the sins of the mother are passed down in verbal, physical and sexual abuse. Behavior that is learned and passed down through the generations causes offspring to feel worthless, like worms. I so often hear people say, "But I am not worthy." This breaks my heart. Victims of abuse tend to feel downtrodden and suffer from very low self-esteem. Broken men and woman visibly portray their pain. I long for them to know that they are worthy through the crucifixion of Jesus Christ who loves them. Sir Winston Churchill, in all humility, once said with such self-assurance, "We are all worms, but I believe I am a glow worm." I so like that, I hope it made you smile!

He (Jesus) *said to them, "Do you bring in a lamp to put it under a bowl or a bed? Instead, don't you put it on its stand?*

43

For whatever is hidden is meant to be disclosed, and whatever is concealed is meant to be brought out into the open. If anyone has ears to hear, let him hear. Mark 4:21-23. Jesus is telling us not to hide light, but to bring it out to where all can see. He is suggesting that what is hidden is meant to be spoken about and what is concealed is to be brought into the light so we can be set free. Most families and marriages have secrets, but abuses need to be brought into the light of truth. Perhaps you have been so downtrodden and haven't lived your life to the fullest, there is help for you. There are people who care. I hear so many stories of abuse on a daily basis. In my experience, healing from abuse is the greatest need among suffering family members. My heart aches for souls suffering from secret "cold" wars in their homes.

I have been involved in the healing ministry since 1990. I thought I was a tough Royal Marine Drill Instructor, but I now feel that my military career was basic training for what the Lord has me doing today, that is, helping others heal. It is astonishing how many people who have suffered horrible abuse are able to get up every morning and function. I minister to so many victims of wars within their own households. I listen as they share their stories of hideous things that took place in the supposed safety of their childhood bedrooms. Abuses done to them by babysitters, uncles, fathers, mothers, family friends, have been recounted to me as their much needed confidante. Many victims have told me that they were warned by their perpetrators that they must never speak of the "secret." The perpetrators had clearly spelled out for them that if they ever told anyone, the victims themselves or their parents or siblings would be killed.

At a recent conference with Dr. Francis and Judith MacNutt, while laying hands on a woman in need of healing prayer, I received a word of knowledge from the Lord. It came as a vision. I saw a closet door open. Standing in the closet was a skeleton. It said, "Thank you Nigel, I have been waiting a very long time to be set free." And then it ran away! When I told the woman what I had seen and heard, she burst into tears, so grateful that the secret of the skeleton had finally been set free. When I saw her the next day at the conference, she looked radiant. When the secret is set free, the power of the perpetrator is gone. God knew this woman's need and cared so much for her that she never had to say aloud what her secret had been. He just took care of it!

The war in the home can be as terrifying as combat, leaving its victims with terrible scars. Children who watch parents argue or physically fight can be as traumatized as soldiers in combat. The diagnosis of PTSD is given to children as well as adults. In my ministry, I also encounter adult victims who, as children, were given over to devilish cults where they were ritually abused on an ongoing basis. These children grow up to be severely damaged adults suffering what is known as satanic ritual abuse (SRA). The effects of such devastating abuse is indescribable. This type of PTSD is officially known as DID or Dissociative Identity Disorder (DSM-IV); formerly known as MPD or Multiple Personality Disorder. The minds of violently and regularly abused people seek new ways to deal with the horror of life by developing new coping skills to survive. Their brains fragment, rather like a hand grenade, into many personalities or alters. Broken men and women who are suffering within this subgroup of PTSD find creative, alternative ways to continue to function as human beings. God uses therapists, healing ministers, and other professionals to put these DID victims back together again. The healing journey involves helping DID victims to integrate or incorporate their fragmented personalities/alters so that their "core" personality can be restored.

Victims have to move through the fear of letting go of those other personalities/alters that have served to protect their 'core" personality. Persons suffering with DID need to be convinced that they are now safe as adults and are no longer subject to the abuse they endured as children. Watching God heal such totally broken people is such a privilege. One dear woman with whom I prayed used to require ninety minutes every morning to shower and dress, because her several personalities/alters had differing opinions and would argue over which soap to use and what clothing to wear. Slowly God healed her, and she is now able to finish her morning routine in just twenty minutes! The healing grace of Christ is made so very obvious in and through answered prayers.

Thankfully God continues to heal distressed people. So many suffer from an ongoing fear of abuse even after the actual threat has gone or the abuser has left or passed away. Like the experiences of a combatant, memories of abuse intensify and fester, haunting victims and creating havoc in their daily life. The root causes of PTSD (the anticipation and fear of the threat of pain or death, either real or perceived) are the same for veterans of war and victims of abuse: children, wives, and even husbands.

I shall never forget the time I took part in a panel discussion at a conference with Francis and Judith MacNutt and several other esteemed colleagues in the healing ministry. Out of the blue, Judith received a word of knowledge from the Lord. Normally light-hearted, her whole demeanor suddenly changed as she announced that there was someone in the room who was being abused by her husband. With anointed authority, Judith boldly urged that this woman must not go home to her abuser. There was a stunned silence as she visually searched the room, hoping to help this victim. Judith knew through God's revelation that this was a very dangerous situation.

So many abused spouses refuse to leave their abusers because of fear. Fear of retribution, fear of loneliness, fear of financial hardship, fear of losing their children, and a variety of other fears. They choose to stay in spite of their fear of pain or, indeed, fear for their very lives, as their ranting and raging spouses, partners, or lovers continue to deliver verbal and/or physical pain to them. In my first book, *Hand to Hand: From Combat to Healing*, I told the story of a woman whose right hand was broken in seven places when her husband pushed her downstairs during an argument on a Sunday. The following Tuesday she came to a healing service that I led and we prayed for her. That same afternoon she paid cash to have an x-ray taken of her hand again, as she believed, by faith, that her broken hand was healed. It was. The x-ray showed no fractures.

This healing had a great impact on me personally. My faith increased a thousandfold. A few weeks later, this woman's doctor telephoned me and asked if I would be willing to testify in court that those seven broken bones had healed after only three days. He told me that bones require six weeks to heal and informed me that the woman's HMO was refusing to pay his bill for her medical treatment, as they did not believe what had happened. I told the doctor that I would be thrilled to testify, not for the sake of the doctor, but for God. I promised to tell the truth, the whole truth, and nothing but the truth, so help me God. Unfortunately they settled out of court, and I never had the opportunity to testify. But praise the Lord, this woman's hand had been miraculously healed after we prayed and together asked God to heal her!

I minister to many men and women over the age of 50 who are ready to unload what happened to them when they were children. They have retained years of stored memories, locked up and hidden, hindering their ability to live freely and leaving them emotionally scarred. Often people become willing to tell their stories to me after the perpetrator has passed away. The shadowy cloud of abuse has been hanging over them for years, convincing them that it cannot be lifted or blown away. Their memories of abuse chain them to the pain of their past; excruciating, palpable pain that remains hidden from the people around them. When they are finally able to share their stories, the clouds part and their chains are broken. Years of shoveling their pain underneath a carpet, out of sight, results in a heap so large that it is tripped over. When that rug is pulled back and all that nasty stuff is exposed and swept clean, that rug can be laid again and they can walk without fear of tripping. Telling their stories makes their paths straight again and restores their lives to them. It is such a privilege to help victims discern between real and perceived power and to recognize that their perpetrators have been rendered powerless. I'll be sharing more about how that happens later.

One of many domestic violence stories I have heard concerns a woman who had vowed, at a young age, that she would never be divorced. She came to my prayer service in the company of her brother and sister, seeking healing from cancer. As I listened to what had brought her to the service, her brother mentioned that her husband was verbally abusive to her. I asked her if it had escalated to physical abuse. The woman looked blankly at the floor as tears ran down her face. Her tears turned into sobs. Her siblings became angry and possessive. Born out of my total dependence upon God in ministry settings, I realized what was really going on with her. I told her that I knew that she would rather die of cancer than be divorced. I also told her, very bluntly, not to go home. I presented the truth because

I know that truth sets us free. She looked at me as if I was the devil incarnate and became very angry. She stormed out of the prayer room, followed closely by her siblings. I sat stunned as I listened to the screeching tires of their car leaving the parking lot. For some while I sat there praying and questioning myself, "Should I have been so blunt?"

I was in such turmoil as I second-guessed myself and what I believed God had shown me. Even after calling my spiritual director, I continued to condemn myself. But God is so wonderful! Just a few days later a guest came to stay from the UK, a doctor who practiced at Burrswood, a Christian hospital in England. I told him what had happened, and he shared a story with me that put my heart at rest on the one hand, while horrifying me on the other. He told me about a lady from Wales who had come to him for prayer. She had confessed that her husband was physically abusive. This doctor had advised her, in no uncertain terms, not to go home. As he recounted this to me, even his posture suggested the authority with which he had spoken to her. He then told me that the following Sunday, he had sat down after lunch to read the newspaper. When he opened it he noticed a photograph of the woman he had met. The headline read, "Woman Killed by Angry Husband Wielding Fireplace Poker." This very sad story put my heart at peace, because I finally knew that I had done the right thing when I had spoken bluntly to the woman who had visited me.

But God is so faithful! This was not the end of my involvement with that woman. Three weeks later the same woman telephoned me to apologize. She shared that she had gone home and thought and prayed about what I had said. "On the third day," she said, "I decided you were right." She realized that, indeed, she had chosen death from cancer rather than divorce. She said that after her husband had gone to work, she packed her personal belongings and left the house. She then told me that she wasn't just calling to apologize and ask me to forgive her rash behavior, but she also wanted me to know that she had since been declared cancer free! She was so excited. The truth had not only set her free from her abuser but also freed her from an inner vow that she would never divorce. Freed from that inner vow, she no longer needed cancer as her way out of an abusive marriage.

Several verses from the Bible come to my mind: *This day I call heaven and earth as witnesses against you that I have set before you life and death, blessings and curses. Now choose life, so that you and your children may live.* Deuteronomy 30:19.

I have chosen the way of truth; I have set my heart on your laws. I hold fast to your statutes, O LORD; do not let me be put to shame. I run in the path of your commands, for you have set my heart free. Psalm 119:30-32

Jesus said to his disciples "Then you will know the truth and the truth will set you free. John 8:32.

Nations of the world have created institutions, such as the United Nations, which are designed to help restore peace to the land. But nations are not alone in declaring war against one another. As we have seen, the family can be a war zone when abuse of any kind is present. Unlike nations, however, wars within families aren't publicly declared; they are kept secret. So who are the peacemakers for our families? I believe that they are our counselors, therapists, doctors, and ministers who serve as healing instruments in the lives of those who suffer. I personally find that among peacemakers, those who know that Truth is a Person named Jesus are the most helpful in healing those who are suffering. *Blessed are the peacemakers, for they will be called sons of God.* Matthew 5:9. Friends, there is help for us. There are many steps along the path to healing, but I am confident that all things are possible in and through Christ.

CHAPTER SIX

The War of the Mind

But I see another law at work in the members of my
body, waging war against the law of my mind
and making me a prisoner of the law of sin
at work within my members.

Romans 7:23

As a child I remember playing with little green plastic men kitted out as soldiers. In my mind's eye, one soldier with a rifle would fire and I would promptly knock down the enemy wearing a gray uniform. The green men always won. Little did I know the truths of war: the lack of food, lack of sleep, lack of comfort, and lack of—well you name it. When I grew to adulthood, this playful fantasy from my childhood became a reality. I learned the truth regarding the actual cause and effect of war. I found out what a Marine sees when he looks down a sniper scope. I learned the effect of pulling the trigger of a rifle. I learned about the death of very real people, not plastic soldiers.

The word "trigger" is frequently used in processing PTSD. The onset of PTSD symptoms is much like a trigger being pulled, releasing a flywheel of stored trauma. It's as if a trigger finger is just waiting for some excuse to release all those unprocessed traumatic memories of the past. Before my healing, something would set me off—a loud noise, a fire alarm, an aggressive person, a situation, or a challenge, and off I would go! The effect on me was troubling: stuttering, incoherence, shaking, confusion, irritability, frustration, and an inability to function. The image of that flywheel would begin spinning freely, gaining momentum with every stressor and traumatic memory that came my way. I just could not function. In those moments, I was transported back into the trauma and was battling for my sanity. In my mind, I begged someone to help me to stop that infernal flywheel from spinning faster and growing larger.

I've read a description of the principle of the flywheel found in the Neolithic spindle and related it to the potter's wheel. I learned that stored energy continues the momentum. In PTSD, stored memory continues the physical and emotional pain just as a flywheel continues the stored momentum of energy. The Bible mentions the imagery of the potter's wheel: *O LORD ... We are the clay, you are the potter; we are all the work of your hand.* Isaiah 68:4. I could add here that we are all cracked pots, some more than others! Some of us have been so buffeted by life's journey that we have been severely damaged. Here is the good news; the Lord repairs those cracks, chips, and breaks. "We have," as my friend Mark Kelso, a singer writes, "been broken to be blessed." Life can break us as God remakes us, according to His will.

Jeremiah 18:3 states: *So I went down to the potter's house, and I saw him working at the wheel. But the pot he was shaping from the clay was marred in his hands; so the potter formed it into another pot, shaping it as seemed best to him.* We, too, can be reworked and healed by "The Potter" as we fly around His wheel. The perfection of His kingdom will come upon us as we place ourselves into the hands of "The Potter." Remake us, dear Lord.

I especially like the analogy of a flywheel when it comes to PTSD. As defined by the Britannica Concise Encyclopedia: *Heavy wheel attached to a rotating shaft to smooth out delivery of power from a motor to a machine. The inertia of the flywheel opposes and moderates fluctuations in the speed of the engine and stores the excess energy for intermittent use.*[1] Personally I see a similarity between the manner in which energy is stored in both a flywheel and a person who is suffering from PTSD. The flywheel is comparable to the workings of a PTSD brain whose speed is at the mercy and regulation of stored traumatic memories. Various stimuli trigger a response in the PTSD victim when powerful energy is drawn from and regulated by the victim's stored traumatic memory.

While I was suffering from shell shock, whenever I was triggered by a noise or smell I felt as though a huge flywheel had been powered up and called for a response. It took a lot of power to get it going, but once it was going it would take up to three days for it to slow down and eventually stop. In my healed condition today that process has been reduced to seconds. Though, in my mind, I can still see a flywheel, it no longer moderates how intensely or how long I will respond when I'm triggered. It is no longer looming over me and operating under its own steam. That flywheel has become very small, the size of a penny; and it no longer regulates my responses. It has lost its power over me. Looking back on how it used to be, I relate to the words found in 2 Peter 2:22: *"A dog returns to its vomit,"* and, *"A sow that is washed returns to her wallowing in the mud."*

I had been a prisoner of my combat memories. But all the while, in the background, "The Potter" was remaking and reshaping this very cracked pot...me! To summarize Romans 7:23: something was waging war against my mind that had made me a prisoner within the confines of my own body. Those memories had power over me; they were all consuming. Still frames and streaming footage of life-

---

[1] http://encyclopedia2.thefreedictionary.com/flywheel

threatening situations got lumped together in my mind and formed a huge mound of garbage that needed to be carted off. Faithful prayer, retelling my story, group therapy sessions, prescribed medications, private meetings with therapists, prayer for inner healing and the healing of memories, were all so important in order to get my right mind back. The many threats on my life, real or perceived, built up over the years to bring me to a total shutdown. I was indeed a prisoner of my tormented mind and I needed to find the key to set me free. The Lord Jesus came to do just that; He was key to my healing. He healed and freed me.

Many therapists liken healing of the past to the peeling of the layers of an onion. As each of the many layers of our lives is peeled away and healed, eventually the very core is reached. Many onion tears accompany this process. I personally prefer to use the analogy of an artichoke when I explain about healing. First you pull off the outer spiked leaves of the artichoke. There is flesh on each of those leaves. Then you continue to work your way from the outside of the plant until you reach the core—the heart of the artichoke, the very heart of healing. That's the prize, the best bit!

The quote from Romans 7 at the beginning of this chapter really gets to the heart of the matter for me where it states: *Waging war against the law of my mind and making me a prisoner of the law.* The war in my mind had been a battle for sanity. It raged against me for a very long time. I had indeed been a prisoner, totally unable to function in daily life because of past issues that had overtaken me. During those painful years, it felt as though the enemy was winning. My past ruled my life and kept my mind in a quagmire of confusion. But slowly over time, the flywheel slowed down and the acute attacks, flashbacks and abreactions, abated. My life eventually returned to normal. Every now and again, my wife can see a mini-flywheel response in me when I begin stuttering slightly. Stuttering used to embarrass me; I felt so weak when it happened. I told Lynn once how it made me feel. She was so kind. She told me that she found it endearing. She said it was "cute." What a kind woman and what a gift to me! The way I perceived it and the way she perceived it were totally different. How important it is to communicate. Just the words "I feel..." can be such a release when an emotion is expressed. Sadly, while in the throes of PTSD, I would shut down and slip into that "thousand-yard stare" where I felt nothing at all. My emotions were so frayed that they just shut down. Over time, with help, those traumatic flashbacks and shutdowns became less frequent and further apart.

In my church's tradition, the Lord's Prayer concludes with these words: *For thine is the kingdom, and the power, and the glory, for ever and ever.* [2] *Amen* ... the power and the glory! In the battle for sanity it helps to face the power of past trauma and reframe it in the light of the Lord's power and glory. Surrendering the power of those horrible memories, exposing them, laying them all out before His power and glory, reduces their power to impact us negatively.

St. Paul wrote in 2 Corinthians 10:5: *We demolish arguments and every pretension that sets itself up against the knowledge of God, and we take captive every thought to make it obedient to Christ.* Be encouraged by these words because, with help, we really can take captive those tormented thoughts of the past and allow them to be healed.

Then there is this bit of wisdom from Proverbs 29:25: *Fear of man will prove to be a snare, but whoever trusts in the LORD is kept safe.* To be allowed to help those trapped in their fear of the past and bring them healed, into the present, is such a privilege.

---

[2] Book of Common Prayer, 1979

The Heavenly Man is the autobiography of Brother Yun, a Chinese national who was imprisoned for seven years for his faith in Christ. Brother Yun once wisely told me, *Do not let your past ruin your present or your future.* That's simple advice but so true. So often the hurts of the past do ruin our present and future. Brother Yun was imprisoned for his faith in Jesus Christ, was tortured and severely beaten, and had both of his legs broken. The mindset that helped him to face each new day during those seven years of imprisonment is summed up in that statement.

As I listen to the stories of traumas suffered from combat, rape, and abuse; I am saddened and often incensed, because I also detect the power that the perpetrators still have over their victims. Even many years later, long after their abusers or their enemies have perhaps forgotten them, their victims continue to suffer pain and anguish. I hear so many stories similar to that of a woman who was sexually abused at eight years of age, who shared her story with me when she was in her fifties. During those fifty years her perpetrator's power had increased. "Perps" often threaten their victims saying, "I will kill your sister or parents if you tell anyone," or "I will kill you if you tell anyone." Frequently victims wait to tell their stories until after the "perp" has died. Another woman recently came to me for prayer, stating that now that her father had died she could tell about the many times he had raped her. Incredibly, she told me that she had not wanted to *embarrass* him while he was still alive. This woman, in finally telling her story, had "defused the bomb" that had been ticking away for years in her mind. The power her father, as perpetrator, had over her and the power of those memories were suddenly deflated, as though a pin had been pushed into a balloon.

By slowing down the flywheel through the telling of the story, the victim realizes that the perpetrator's power is reduced and even negated. The skeleton in the closet of the mind is free to leave, the dark clouds are scattered, and that nasty mound of memories is carted off, when the light of Christ is shone upon it. The light of Jesus exposes the truth and gives us His perspective as He sets us free. After all, Jesus Christ came to set the captives free. Victims become so captive to painful memories of the past and to unforgiveness. But Jesus promises to set us free!

Today we have the benefit of the Critical Incident Debriefing (CID), which is vital to the healing process. As soon as possible after an incident of trauma, a CID team flies into action and helps the victim unpack the event. CID is now offered to first responders, for example, after they have assisted in the aftermath of a multiple-car pileup. Witnessing such trauma is overwhelming and the sooner the unpacking begins, the better. Sadly, I often hear stories that are many years old from the victims who come to me for help. The more time between the incident and the unpacking, the more powerful the memories become. There is a saying that time heals all wounds. Though that may be true of physical wounds, it is not true of traumatic wounds.

Rose Fitzgerald Kennedy (mother of John, Bobby, and Ted) bore the deaths of half of her family before her own demise at age 104. She lost her first born in WWII; her second and seventh born to assassins' bullets; her fourth born in a plane crash; her third born underwent a failed lobotomy, was rendered incapacitated, and was institutionalized. Rose outlived her husband by thirty six years and lived to mourn the deaths of several grandchildren and grieve for various other personal tragedies. Intimately familiar with trauma and the pain of emotional wounds, Rose Kennedy is quoted as having said, *It has been said, 'time heals all wounds.' I do not agree. The wounds remain. In time, the mind, protecting its sanity, covers them with scar tissue and the pain lessens.*

But it is never gone.

Indeed, anyone who has suffered any form of trauma recognizes that the pain festers and gets worse over time. With help, there is even more than hope; healing is available. Perhaps you have been carrying a burden, a secret forced upon you, something that has been quietly burning in your heart for years. Now may be the right time to unburden yourself and unpack that emotional wound. As you consider whether now is the time for you, think on these words: *There is a time for everything, and a season for every activity under heaven: a time to be born and a time to die, a time to plant and a time to uproot, a time to kill and a time to heal, a time to tear down and a time to build, a time to weep and a time to laugh, a time to mourn and a time to dance, a time to scatter stones and a time to gather them, a time to embrace and a time to refrain, a time to search and a time to give up, a time to keep and a time to throw away, a time to tear and a time to mend, a time to be silent and a time to speak, a time to love and a time to hate, a time for war and a time for peace.* Ecclesiastes 3:1-8.

Chapter Seven

Depression

All day long I have been plagued; I have been punished
every morning.
If I had said, "I will speak thus," I would have
betrayed your children.
When I tried to understand all this, it was oppressive
to me
till I entered the sanctuary of God; then I understood
their final destiny.
Psalm 73:14-17

Remember; if you blow a fuse, you will be in the dark.
J. John

A huge part of the war against PTSD is the battle against depression. Psalm 73 is apparently devoted to depression and its healing. It is amazing how God works. As I write this chapter, I've just been advised by my physician that my lungs may be compromised for the rest of my life! To be quite honest, I am struggling with a bit of depression right now. I had been doing rather well in my recuperation from that bout with H1N1 a year or so ago. But yesterday's conversation with the doctor threw me for a loop. To combat the onset of depression, I am saying to myself, "Nigel, this is God's book. Keep writing! Don't let yourself go back to that place you were too familiar with in the mid-1970s when 'the dark night of the soul' lasted far too long." The effects of shell shock, literally shock wave damage to the brain from being too close to an explosion (or in my case, five of them) can cause brain damage. The depression that attaches itself to this diagnosis is like the analogy of the artichoke in the healing process I wrote of in the last chapter. Depression becomes yet another layer of those fleshy, spiked leaves of the plant that must be dealt with as we work from the outside toward the core; the very heart of healing. Depression is a very dark hellhole in the mind and heart. I have prayed with thousands of people suffering from this hellish, destructive struggle. My favorite saint, St. Thérèse of Lisieux, said, *I want to spend my heaven doing good on earth.* Perhaps that could be a starting place for the journey of healing out of the abyss of depression.

Years ago I had a vision about depression. It appeared to me like a tube, two feet in diameter, leading right into the bowels of the earth, into hell itself. Around the edge of the tube was a track wide enough for a billiard ball. At the top of the tube, parked behind a gate and waiting to be released, was a black billiard ball. When something triggered me, the ball was released. Then it began its journey into hell, slowly at first, then gaining momentum. Faster and faster it would descend until it disappeared into the darkness where it festered in that hellish abyss. While I was in the process of my own healing from depression, I repeatedly saw this vision in my mind. Eventually I would see the right hand of Christ appear in this vision near the bottom of the tube as He stopped that ball in its tracks. Over time as I was healing, the position of His hand would move further up, inching closer and closer to the release gate at the top of the tube. Finally one day, Christ's hand touched the gate! Though I had triggered the release of that gate, this time Jesus' hand held the ball in place, stopping it from rolling down ever again. It was at that moment that I was delivered from depression. (As I write this chapter the Chile mine rescue is in progress. The rescue shaft drilled into the earth is not unlike the vision I saw years ago. In this case the miners were rescued after ten weeks underground).

Many years later that deliverance would be put to the test. At that time I was in a situation where I *wanted* to revisit that dark place in my mind and wallow in depression once again. I felt I had very good reasons to feel that way. I could readily qualify and quantify the essence of the cause. The trigger was valid. All the ingredients were in place for a jolly good session of depression. I went into a chapel to wallow in my misery, but what happened astounded me. I *tried* to get depressed. I *wanted* to be depressed, because I had good reason to be. But I just sat there and laughed. Depression was the very last thing on my mind. I then realized that the dark, familiar place I had known so well had gone for good. I could not be depressed! I actually laughed out loud. The verses from Psalm 73:16-17 spoke to me: *When I tried to understand all this, it was oppressive to me till I entered the sanctuary of God; then I understood...* I had entered the sanctuary (the chapel) in an oppressive state of mind, and then I understood what was going on. My laughter had resulted from the revelation that the Lord had already lifted depression from me and I could not go back there, even if I wanted to.

What had happened? On numerous occasions, the New International Version of the Bible uses the expression, *I looked and I saw.* Well, "I looked and I saw" a room in my mind. It was a dark and disheveled room, dirty and slimy. The carpet was raised off the floor, exposing all the "stuff" I had swept under it. The room was a total mess. All of the unpleasant, negative facets of my life had been stored in this one room. It was not a nice place! Then "I looked and I saw" a mighty cleanup crew of angels entering with shovels as they dug out what needed to be discarded. Then more angels came with steam cleaners and scoured the room. They were followed by a team of angelic designers armed with clip boards and plans to revamp the room. Then came builder angels who installed a huge Palladian window as they transformed my squalid man-cave into a well-appointed study. They also mounted a huge-flat screen television, put in a very nice brown leather recliner, and painted the walls, deep green. My man-cave had been given a holy make-over by God. That part of my brain that had once been governed by depression, had been converted from a dark, dank place into a delightful den of reflection. My wife even had a phone installed so that she could reach me at any time! As the vision ended, "I looked and I saw" again that I had been healed of chronic depression! I had been set free. Jesus Christ had come to set this captive free. The oppression had gone. My brain had been rewired by God Himself.

For many years since, I have laid my hands upon the heads of countless people and prayed for the healing of emotional and mental problems in their brains. I pray that others will experience God's rewiring of their minds as I have. Oftentimes I envision an old-fashioned telephone operator advising callers, "I am trying to connect you." The comedy sketch ("One RingyDingy") made famous by Lily Tomlin comes to mind, as she would franticly try to connect many phone lines ringing in at once. Then one day I happened to notice a newspaper headline that read, "Brain rewires itself." I bought the paper and read about a man who had been in a coma for many years. One day he simply woke up. He had to learn how to speak again, but he woke up. Did God rewire his brain? That article made sense of my practice to ask God, in prayer, to heal brains by rewiring them.

In December 2008 I had the privilege of visiting a

children's hospital to pray for the patients. I was with Sister Mary Elizabeth, a nun from the Community of St. Mary of Greenwich, NY. The first night we led a healing service there. The next day Sister and I were invited to go on rounds with the chaplain and a couple of nurses. As a team we prayed for children with all sorts of concerns, including those with Shaken Baby Syndrome. It was very sad. Some children spent their days strapped to a board tilted slightly downward. The physical and emotional circumstances of each child were heart-wrenching. It felt as though these patients were parked in a sort of long-term lot designated for those who could not function in daily life.

As our team went from room to room, I fought back tears. In one room I saw an older boy, head slumped, sitting in a wheel chair. His eyes were closed. We laid hands on the lad and I anointed his head. I made the sign of the cross with oil on his forehead. And then, as is my custom with brain issues, I continued to anoint his head all the way around, praying aloud, "Jesus wore a crown of thorns, may you wear a crown of crosses." I was three-quarters of the way around when I came upon an indent in his skull. I anointed the center of the indent, and while I was praying for godly and holy rewiring, he woke up. A Jewish social worker standing near us fell to her knees and, raising her hands to the heavens, began praising God. Suddenly the chaplain ran out of the room. General panic broke out. I just stood there, confused and in shock. I tried to ask, "What's happening?", but no one responded for quite a while. Finally I was informed that this young man had been in a car crash and had been comatose for four years. The lad had apparently just then come out of the coma. Many of us, myself included, had tears streaming down our cheeks as we were joined by others who had come running to witness what had happened. God had rewired this lad's brain as he was being anointed. We were all in awe and, to be honest, I still am. I will remember this miracle for the rest of my life. The power of prayer with God's anointing is incomparable. The very moment that boy was anointed at the concave center point of the indent in his head (perhaps the actual point of impact during the crash), he awoke! God had rewired his brain and healed him before our very eyes. All who had gathered in His Name were privileged as "we looked and we saw!"

Clearly I am persuaded that this godly rewiring can, and does, happen in the brain. If God can awaken people from the deepest coma, I believe that He can rewire our brains to deliver us from depression. One of the biggest things I have learned since my sister, Julie Sheldon, was miraculously healed in 1989 is that we must not limit God. In her book, *Dancer Off Her Feet*,[3] Julie recounts the astounding healing that God blessed her with, restoring her in body, mind, and spirit. I confess and deeply regret my lack of faith in the past as I limited my expectations of God's power. We need to pray bigger, think bigger, and believe bigger. My dear friend and mentor, Dr. Francis MacNutt often reminds us, *People are dying because people are not praying for them.* I know that I am alive because people prayed for me. I know that I was delivered from depression because of prayer. I know that He resurrects the dead, raises the comatose, restores our health, and redeems our minds.

If one or both of your parents struggle(d) with depression, might you have learned from them how to be depressed if you also suffer from depression? Are you living with a spouse who is depressed? Have faith and pray; and pray some more. Keep praying, do not quit. Allow my story

---

[3] Hodder and Stoughton, London

of that comatose child to heal your unbelief. The onus of faith for prayer is not upon the one in need of healing (the "supplicant"), but upon those others who are praying for the supplicant. For it is by faith that we are healed, the shared faith of all those who are praying. It certainly is helpful if the supplicant also has faith, but the pooled faith of the prayer team, as they assemble on their knees, is vital. Take comfort in the words of the prophet Isaiah 9:2: *The people walking in darkness have seen a great light; on those living in the land of deep darkness a light has dawned.* (NIV©2010); as well as the words of Christ as found in John 8:12: *When Jesus spoke again to the people, he said, "I am the light of the world. Whoever follows me will never walk in darkness, but will have the light of life."*

If you or someone you love is struggling with depression, my prayer is that God will rewire your hurting, darkened minds as the *light of the world* illuminates your paths toward healing and the ability to once again *have the light of life.*

CHAPTER EIGHT

Collateral Damage, Collateral Healing

*Let every priest receive the money
from one of the treasurers,
and let it be used to repair whatever
damage is found in the temple.*

2 Kings 12:5

*In war: Resolution
In defeat: Defiance
In victory: Magnanimity
In peace: Goodwill*

Sir Winston Churchill

The words "collateral damage" are often used by the media in regard to war, as a catch-all phrase for the residual effects of battle. It is generally regarded that the first use of this phrase was in reference to the atomic bombings of Japan in WWII. It was also used extensively in the Vietnam war in reference to "friendly fire" (fellow combatants killed by the same side or the killing of non-combatants). Wikipedia defines collateral damage as *damage that is unintended or incidental to the intended outcome.* The United States Air Force defines the term as *[the] unintentional damage or incidental damage affecting facilities, equipment, or personnel, occurring as a result of military actions directed against targeted enemy forces or facilities. Such damage can occur to friendly, neutral, and even enemy forces.*[4]

Intent seems to be the key element in understanding the military definition of collateral damage as it relates to target selection and prosecution. It is damage aside from that which was intended. In an article written just prior to the USA's involvement in the Iraq war, U.S. Secretary of Defense Donald Rumsfeld stated, *If force becomes necessary, it is clear that coalition forces would take great care to avoid civilian casualties.* In the same article a senior U.S. Central Command official explained, *collateral damage can take two forms: injuries or deaths among noncombatants and damage to property. It is important to remember, he noted, that it's nearly impossible to eliminate collateral damage. Weapon systems malfunctions, human error and "the fog of war" all contribute.*[5] The widening use of this term, and the way it serves to undermine or neutralize the trauma of what it defines, were evident in an interview of Timothy McVeigh before his execution for the Oklahoma City Federal Building bombing in April 1995. McVeigh, a Gulf War veteran, referred to the deaths of 19 children, who were among the 168 who died, as "collateral damage."[6]

I see returning veterans who suffer with PTSD as collateral damage as well. In fact, many who have been emotionally traumatized in combat also impact those around them with their collateral damage as they return from the battlefront

---

[4] USAF Intelligence Targeting Guide—AIR FORCE PAMPHLET 14-210 Intelligence. 1998-02-01. p. 180.

[5] "U.S. Military Works to Eliminate Civilian Deaths, Collateral Damage" http://www.defense.gov/news/newsarticle.aspx?id=29337.

[6] "Orwell Would Revel in 'Collateral Damage'" Ibish, Los Angeles Times, Apr. 9, 2001. http://www.commondreams.org/views01/0409-03.htm.

into their homes. Their spouses are affected, their children are affected, and all other people around them are affected. Returning combatants are not the same as they were before they left for battle; they are physically and emotionally different. Personally I didn't recognize this when I returned from my first tour of combat duty. Twenty-twenty hindsight is helpful as I reflect on this now; but as a teen recruit back then I thought I was invincible. I could not imagine that I would ever be affected by a bullet or a bomb, or by applying field bandages to the rasping wound of a fellow Marine, or by hearing the last cry of a Marine dying.

In December 2008 I led a three day retreat for therapists, physiotherapists, psychologists, and psychiatrists in Boston, teaching them how to help and pray with combat veterans. On the "third day" I was having lunch with ten doctors when suddenly I had a flashback, an abreaction. I hadn't had one since 1982. I was shocked as my mind transported me back thirty-six years to a "contact" situation when I patrolled the streets of Belfast in 1972. As we prepared to cross a street intersection, I had just glanced at the patrol leader, my good friend Tim Shayler, I heard a loud report of gunfire, and saw Tim fall to the ground. He reported the contact, "Agh, I've been hit." Those words still resound in my head all these years later. We all loaded our weapons and took cover, expecting a full-on firefight. "What can I shoot at? Where is a target?" I lay there just waiting to be shot, without a target to fire at. "What will the round feel like? Where will it hit me?" So much went through my mind. All my military training was put to use in seconds. "What will it feel like? What can I shoot at? Will the round pass through me or hit a bone, ricochet, and tumble through my body? Where is a target? Will it put out my eye? Where is a target? Will I feel the pain? Where is a target? I want to pull the trigger."

Looking back on that flashback in 2008 as I sat with those doctors in Boston, I could not share with them these thoughts from 1972 that remained unspoken, but graphically described how I felt. Those words were too personal, and I feared that they would open me to the criticism and condemnation of others. Many combatants have problems telling their stories to civilian therapists who have never been in combat because they fear condemnation. This fear can be a huge block to healing. Since this occurred in 1972, I had never spoken the words that I have just written, to anyone. Fearing judgment by those who have never been in my situation, I remained silent. Even now having written them, my insides are shaking just as they were almost forty years ago.

The flashback continued as I relived seeing my friend Tim lying on the ground in a huge pool of blood. An armored Saracen ambulance arrived and carried him away. I was sickened to the core as I watched four teenagers dance in Tim's blood, shouting: "Another F#!*#*! British solider has been killed." My blood was boiling. I so wanted to open fire on them. "That is my friend's blood," I wanted to shout. One arm pulled my rifle one way and my other arm pulled it in the direction of the lads kicking Tim's blood all over the street. In all the years since this event happened, I had never shared this memory. As I sat at the table with those doctors in Boston, I felt all the anxiety from that moment. I began to sweat profusely as this flashback played out.

Then suddenly everything changed! In my mind I was now looking at those teenagers while lying next to a building across the street from them. But this time I saw the Lord standing with the teens in Tim's blood. He was looking at me as if He was trying to get my attention. He spoke saying, "Nigel, it is time to forgive these lads." I was so shocked. He then looked down at the teens and said to them, "This man, Tim, was made in My image. This is My blood you are kicking around. Stop it!" With the Lord present, the memory was healed in a moment. I felt a huge burden rise from my shoulders as this debilitating memory was healed by the Lord.

Why am I telling you this story? Perhaps you also have memories that need to be healed. Perhaps your mind reels as mine did, having witnessed the horrors of man's inhumanity to man. I want you to know that all things are possible in and through Jesus Christ, Who is still in the business of healing. Something always happens when we pray. I know that the prayers of many people brought me through my recent illness of the H1N1 virus. I am alive today because our Lord Jesus Christ raised me. I pray that you will not carry around the burden of an unhealed memory in the years to come.

The collateral damage in Tim's journey, however, began when his wife stood by the kitchen sink and watched as a police car parked in front of their house. Two police officers stepped out of the squad car. She instantly knew what that meant. This was the moment all spouses feared and dreaded: the messengers of doom had arrived. There was a knock at the door. And she began to miscarry. Tim's child was lost in the stress of that moment and, eventually, so was his marriage. That is collateral damage, and all too often it goes unreported and unrecognized as such. Tim was shot, but his child died!

Do you not know that your body is a temple of the Holy Spirit, who is in you, whom you have received from God? You are not your own. 1 Corinthians 6:19. So often the body has been abused by either physical or visual traumas which are so atrocious that they require long-term healing. The verse at the start of this chapter from 2 Kings 12:5: *Let every priest receive the money from one of the treasurers, and let it be used to repair whatever damage is found in the temple.* (Emphasis added) addresses the damage found in the "physical place of worship"—our bodies. The physical and emotional damage from trauma affects not only the victim, but all those around the victim as well. The collateral damage of PTSD is experienced by the victim's entire circle of family and friends; and the residual effect in the continuation of the war of the mind is evident to many of them. Repairing the damage of the "temple" is vitally important, and entirely possible.

Survivor's guilt also comes under this heading of collateral damage. Evidence of survivor's guilt is often heard in statements such as, "I should have died with them," or "If only I...perhaps I could have saved his life." Survivor's guilt, or survivor's syndrome, is a condition that occurs when a person perceives himself to have done wrong by surviving a traumatic event where others did not. This condition may be found among survivors of combat, natural disasters, epidemics, among friends and family in the aftermath of a suicide, and even in business among those who are retained when their co-workers are laid off. The experience and manifestation of survivor's guilt will depend on an individual's psychological profile. Interestingly, Wikipedia reports that when the Diagnostic and Statistical Manual of Mental Disorders IV (DSM-IV) was published, survivor's guilt was removed as a recognized separate diagnosis, and was redefined as a significant symptom of post-traumatic stress disorder (PTSD).

This condition is prevalent in survivors following a suicide, who may have missed a friend's weekly phone call "that" night; when "that" night was the very night that their friend killed himself. I have heard survivors describe this very scenario to me and have seen how it damages them. Perhaps the survivor missed warning signs or failed to give them credence. This associated guilt can be all-consuming. Help is needed to bring survivors slowly into the truth: there was nothing that the survivor could have done to prevent the suicide. The Bible says, *Then you will know the truth, and the truth will set you free.* (John 8:32) By unpacking the event and finding the real truth, survivors can be brought into greater understanding and peace. As he or she realizes the truth, the burden no longer needs to be carried. Until then, however, the magnitude of internalized self-condemnation and guilt that survivors feel makes for a very tough battle. As I minister to those who are yet caught in this self-sacrificial state of mind, I am reminded that our Lord was sacrificed for us that we might live and have life abundantly. When survivor's guilt is lifted with the help of well-trained therapists and prayer teams, captives are set free! Such traumatic entries in our mental diaries hold us captive until we discover ways in which we can be set free from their horror.

At the start of my first book, *Hand to Hand: From Combat to Healing*, I described an incident that happened in the early 1970s when a fellow Marine and I were cornered in a back alley. Down the next sector of the alley, we saw a man with a machine gun. Our training required that we read a warning to him, a script written on a yellow card which we were carrying. If we had obeyed that we might have been mown to bits by his machine gun. In less than a second a decision had to be made. Do we shoot or do we hold our fire? Do we give the command to halt and risk certain death?

My uncle, whom I deeply respect, Group Captain Anthony Mumford (43 Squadron Flight Command, RAF, Deputy leader of the Queens Flight, decorated for flying Hunters in the Korean war and saving a company of Royal Marines), said to me upon reading this account in my first book, "Mumford, you should have shot the b-----d!" Perhaps I should have. But to this day I don't know whether that man went on to shoot others. Nor do I know if he was one of us, one of our own in the next sector. It was dusk and hard to make out his uniform, though the machine gun he was carrying was in clear sight. That same gun was carried by NCOs so he could have been an NCO, though he was not wearing any identifiable head covering. Was he a terrorist? Should we have shot him? All these questions still haunt me. Years later, there was even a brief time after my uncle's admonishment, when survivor's guilt set in and I believed that I should have shot him. But now that I am a priest, I am very grateful that I did not.

I cannot recall the name of my fellow Marine in the alley, though we both lay together either side of that alley, on the ground with our eyes trained on that machine gunner. One well-aimed shot on his part could have taken us out, just as a well-aimed shot from me could have taken him out. Then a dog barked, which broke the tension, and the gunner slipped into the shadows. Gone! Perhaps he, too, had weighed the situation and decided it was a stalemate. Is the guilt still there? Yes. But do I feel released from it now? Yes. Is there self-condemnation for not pulling the trigger? Not any longer. I have put my trust in the Lord, and I believe that in that situation my lack of action was correct. Is there any residual to this memory? Yes, a pinch of something. But now the bottom line: I am very glad I did not shoot him. He may have been one of us in the next sector, doing the very same thing as we were. Had I pulled that trigger and later discovered that I'd caused a "friendly fire" incident and produced "collateral damage," that would have been very tough to live with. I will likely never know the truth unless that chap on the other end of my rifle scope reads this book and contacts me!

In this chapter, we have taken a look at collateral damage in light of combat and other traumatic events. But when we observe it in peacetime, we must change its name to "collateral healing." Collateral damage can be evidenced in something as simple as a sneeze. The germs are passed on. Contagious and infectious diseases get passed on inadvertently. Similarly, I believe healing is often passed on in the same manner. I observe collateral healing in the Welcome Home Initiatives (WHI) that I lead several times a year at the Spiritual Life Center in Greenwich, NY. Combatants gather from many theaters of war and find healing among those who have been in the same situation. I also witness collateral healing in the gatherings of people who attend the healing services I celebrate weekly, as well as during healing missions that I lead across the country. The healing grace of God is contagious at such gatherings. People "catch" the joy and "catch" the healing grace of God, just as we are prone to "catch" a cold! When we gather with like-minded people, those seeking healing of some sort, God's grace abounds in us. In those gatherings, the weight of our burdens is shared and they become lighter.

In St. Paul's letter to the Galatians, chapter 6, verse 2, he wrote: *Carry each other's burdens, and in this way you will fulfill the law of Christ.* When you gather with others in community, the burden is not all upon your shoulders. Excerpts from some of St. Paul's use of "others" in the Bible gives us further insight into healing. *You, my brothers, were called to be free...serve one another in love.* (Galatians 5:13). And, *Be completely humble and gentle; be patient, bearing with one another in love.* (Ephesians 4:2). Also, *Bear with each other and forgive whatever grievances you may have ... Forgive as the Lord forgave you.* (Colossians 3:13). And finally, *Therefore encourage one another and build each other up,* (1 Thessalonians 5:11).

It is so wonderful to see this healing phenomenon as former combatants gather in friendship and camaraderie with others during our Welcome Home Initiatives. The same is also true during gatherings of first responders, or of alcoholics, or of any group when people are seeking help. Our need for friendship and common ground, for a "safe place" to tell our stories, is a basic human need. We have been pre-wired by our Creator to love, forgive, serve, encourage, build up, and bear with one another in order to help free one another from the shackles of our human condition. That is healing! It is found whenever we gather together in settings where we are safe and can be vulnerable to receive from one another. The realization that we are not alone; that God is with us; that others have suffered as we have in similar situations and experiences, is often the first step toward healing. It is within this framework that collateral healing can redeem collateral damage.

CHAPTER NINE

September 11, 2001: The Nation and the World Need Healing

In the day of great slaughter, when the towers fall, streams of water will flow on every high mountain and every lofty hill. The moon will shine like the sun, and the sunlight will be seven times brighter, like the light of seven full days, when the LORD binds up the bruises of his people and heals the wounds.

Isaiah 30:25-26

The whole international community will be united in condemning what they have done.

NATO Secretary
General Lord Robertson

As for those that carried out these attacks there are no adequate words of condemnation. Their barbarism will stand as their shame for all eternity.

British Prime Minister Tony Blair

I fear that all I have done is awakened a sleeping giant and filled him with a terrible resolve.

Admiral Yamamoto after the Pearl
Harbor attack, December 7, 1941

September 11, 2001: a day that we all remember! That fateful morning changed everything for us. Most people remember what they were doing that day, just as many still remember what they were doing when President John F. Kennedy was shot. In 1963, I was nine years old and was at boarding school, standing next to a fire bell, when I heard the news about JFK's death. I remember that moment vividly. Events such as these invariably create a need for personal and even national healing.

The destruction of the World Trade Center was shown on television over and over again, traumatizing the entire nation with shock and horror. I remember my first visit to the World Trade Center in 1978. I stood in long lines wending around the first floor, waiting to take the express elevator to the top. I can still vividly recall the beautiful view from the top. But my memories were changed in an instant on that fateful day in 2001. I was getting ready for the weekly Tuesday healing service in Kent, Connecticut. I had been writing that morning before the service began and had not heard any news until people came into the church. Initially they came with confused reports, but as more people arrived, the depth of the horror began to unfold. We all stood in a circle and prayed. Was this doomsday? People were weeping. Fear and concern were evident in all, but we persevered in prayer as people were perishing in New York City. There were long periods of quiet interrupted only by intermittent sobbing. We left the church around noon and watched the devastation as it was endlessly reported on television.

Mainland America was under attack! Our nation was worried about the "next hit." A war began. And that hopeful salutation, "Peace and goodwill to all mankind," was left hanging like Christ Himself on the cross. The nation was hit by the full force of PTSD. Raw trauma filled the streets and every household in America. Along with the absolute devastation of the largest landmark in the USA came the menacing message to every citizen: the enemy means business. All the people in the Twin Towers and on the streets of New York City were so violently traumatized. And so were all of us who watched on our televisions. As I write this I can feel the same emotions as I did then. You might also be feeling them right now as you remember that day. I felt an onslaught of stress. Butterflies flew at the base of my sternum. Right now I am actually wondering whether you will even want to read this, choosing to skip it and go on to the next chapter. You may not want to recollect those images yet again, preferring to avoid the whole experience. If you do, please know that your reaction is normal. It is evidence that we need healing from such an unprecedented trauma. We want to say, "You know I really don't want to be reminded of this." This national tragedy has left a gaping wound in the lives of millions of people. My hope is that you'll choose to read on so that healing from this catastrophic event can come.

I received an email that fateful day at 8:47.56 a.m. The first plane hit the north tower at 8.45 a.m. This email sent nearly three minutes later read, "Please say a prayer. It has been reported that a plane has hit the World Trade Center. I can see the smoke from my office." I still have that email; it is now framed and hangs on my wall.

Four days later, on September 15, 2001, Lynn and I got married. Since all aircraft were grounded, just a few of our long-distance family and friends could make it to the wedding. Fortunately, my parents had flown from the UK on September 10. My father had pointed out the Twin Towers to my mother as they traveled from the airport by car and crossed over a bridge with a view of the New York skyline. The next day the towers were gone! When I asked my rector if Lynn and I should pick another wedding date, he said with patriotic resolve, "Illegitimis non carborundum est!" (*Don't let the b-----ds grind you down!*) To make our wedding day even more poignant, my best man and brother, Alec, was grounded in the UK. I had to find a number two best man. My good friend Larry Brion, himself a grounded pilot, became my best man. He wore his pilot's uniform and as he gave the wedding toast, it was a very moving experience for all of us. The events of 9/11 (a name by which it is now known) hung heavily over us on this very special day of our life.

A month after the wedding, I was asked to go to "Ground Zero" to minister to anyone who needed prayer. I was given a phone number to call in order to get through the military cordon. As my wife and I drove down the Henry Hudson Highway we became very aware that something was missing. We drove in silence for several miles, until my bride said aloud, "Seeing the new skyline must be similar to when a woman looks in the mirror after a mastectomy." We both wept silently.

After parking the car north of Canal Street I had to walk several blocks to the bomb site. The stench was overpowering. A pungent mixture of concrete dust and rotting flesh, an odor I shall never forget and pray I will never smell again. All my combat experiences flooded back in that walk of several blocks. It was silent and still; no one was there. It was like a ghost town. When I arrived at the military cordon at St. Paul's Chapel, I made the phone call and was allowed past the military into the chapel. I was given a tour by the young woman who was in charge of the volunteers. There were exhausted men and women in uniforms in the pews: lying, sleeping, and talking in hushed tones. At the back wall was a pile of boots with burnt soles from the still smoldering pile of what was left of the towers. I realized that terror had also burnt through the very souls of these selfless volunteers. I was led halfway up the back stairs of St. Paul's by this young woman when she stopped and opened a window that overlooked the smoking pile of rubble (the "pile" would later be called the "pit"). I shall never forget the horror of the disgusting odor that came through the window, the same stench as before but so much stronger. It was the very smell of death and destruction. As I looked out, the graveyard of St. Paul's was a surreal scene of gray dust several feet deep, but not one church window was broken or cracked! That alone was an incredible miracle.

I stood on those stairs listening to the voices and other strains of those still looking for bodies. As something was found, the site became silent. We stood for a very long time in a trancelike state, unable to fully comprehend it all. Our silence was broken when my guide, this young woman, began to pour out all that she had been through. I found myself part of an unplanned critical incident debriefing (CID). I said nothing. I simply listened, not wanting to make any noise whatsoever. It became a prayer session that I shall never forget. She had seen it all, had been in it, and was now helping others on the front line. Her calm persona amazed me, but also worried me, for this was the first time she had shared about what she had experienced. She went into great detail, even describing what had happened to the "jumpers," those who had plunged to their death from the burning buildings. All the while, her eyes were transfixed on that "pile" of still smoldering debris (which went on to burn for three months). We stood there for hours as I listened. The fortitude of this young hero, in the midst of death and destruction, was awe-inspiring. She deeply touched my soul that day. We concluded with prayer. We prayed for inner healing and the healing of memories.

While I was still there, a great silence suddenly fell upon the site. A woman's left forearm and hand had been found with a wedding ring still on her finger. It was intensely moving. Tears began to spill from everyone's eyes, especially the eyes of those battle-fatigued and weary firemen who were working around the clock to rescue whatever remains they could find. After a very long day and many heartrending conversations, I finally met up with my dear wife and together we drove back to Kent. I was somewhat broken. No, that's a typical British understatement! I was completely broken! Again I had looked into the face of terror and I felt utterly spent.

The next day I turned on the air conditioning in my car and got a face full of ash as my nostrils filled with that putrid stench I had smelt the day before. I pulled off the road and wept... for a long time. There I was left in my own crushing grief. Then I realized that I'd only spent one day there and felt so devastated. How were the relatives and friends of those who had perished feeling about their losses? How were the volunteer rescue workers and paid service personnel coping with what they saw day after day? My soul was pierced as an overpowering delayed grief poured over me. As I write this now and recall the events of that day, I pray that the young woman who was my guide that day is now prospering in her life. I also pray for the repose of the very souls whom I breathed in that day.

I don't know about you, but I need to take a break now and make myself a cup of tea. I'm dealing with memories that I haven't thought about for ten years. Memories of a day that feels like it was just yesterday. Perhaps you'd like a break now, too? Tea can be so healing. So British, but so healing! So go boil a kettle. Go on—'ave a cuppa!

For about three years after the 9/11 trauma I met with many people who were directly or indirectly involved with the Twin Towers tragedy. An elderly British man came to me from a church in Connecticut. He was suffering with the full symptoms of PTSD. He had been a FOO, Forward Observation Officer, who brought in fire from the artillery during WWII.

He hadn't suffered any symptoms since the war, but he had experienced a total breakdown when he read the New York Times 9/11 headlines, "Three Thousand People Lose Their Lives." The news hit him right between the eyes. He estimated that he had killed about three thousand people during the Second World War as he brought in ordnance upon them. He had gone all those years managing a normal life until that headline caused major collateral damage in his mind. He had been made very deaf during the war, due to the noise of artillery, so it was difficult to pray with him. But the Lord made a way for me to introduce him to the healing of memories, allowing him to be freed from his guilt and anxiety.

The collapse of the World Trade Center towers has been called *the most infamous paradigm* of progressive collapse. [7] Indeed, I saw that progressive collapse in that dear WWII war veteran who broke down after reading those headlines. It was as if a bullet had finally hit him, all those years later, and I watched him buckle, right in front of me, just as those towers had.

The mind's capacity for dealing with disaster fascinates me. How do we carry on our "normal" lives after such devastation? "Carrying on" is what the survivors of the Blitz in London did, in the early 1940s, with resolve, perseverance, and grit. It just wasn't spoken about. The Blitz went on, and they just picked themselves up and carried on, as though it hadn't happened. Perhaps because I also didn't discuss my trauma story and its impact on me, I am so amazed at their stiff-upper-lip demeanor. In my case, when

---

[7] Zdenk P. Bažant and Mathieu Verdure. "Mechanics of Progressive Collapse: Learning from World Trade Center and Building Demolitions" J. Engrg. Mech. Vol. 133:3, pp. 308-19. March 2007.

I was triggered, it was as if an alarm had sounded, signaling danger, and off I would go again! How people simply get up the next morning and live "normally" despite having been so severely traumatized, perplexes me. Somehow human beings learn to carry on despite the huge, but invisible, scar they bear from extreme trauma. But no matter how "normal" they may appear, eventually that wound will surface and will come to light in strange behavior. My best friend's father, for example, was one of the first British officers to enter Bergen-Belsen concentration camp at the end of WWII. He was never the same after that. Though he had put on a façade in an effort to conceal his unseen scar, that wound was just too great to hide. His temperament was disrupted by the great angst he internalized following his return home. Though he appeared to be a tough guy outwardly, he was a very broken man inside.

How then do we cope with a history of individual and/ or national trauma?

A certain woman for whom I prayed had a great effect on me. Two years after 9/11, on the morning of the day that Lynn and I were to fly to the UK, we had a visit from this woman. She told me that it had taken her two years to pluck up the courage to come and ask for prayer. She then proceeded to share with me that her daughter had been a flight attendant on American Airlines Flight 11, the first plane that hit the North Tower at 8.45 a.m. These are her very words she said to me, "We were lucky. We found her left forearm and wedding ring."

I lost it. I simply fell apart. Remember, I had been at the "pile" at St. Paul's Chapel, when they found her arm! And here I was, two full years later, talking to her Mum. Coincidence or God-incidence? She was such a broken mother. Our time of prayer and the healing of memories helped her. When I told her that I was on site when they found her daughter's arm, she was greatly comforted. I remained in contact with her for several years following our visit. The collateral damage to her family was so very sad. And her words, "We were lucky…" still echo in my mind. In those words, I recognized that this precious mother was aware that most relatives had nothing to bury of their loved ones who perished that day. Though her flight attendant daughter had died, she could still say, "We were lucky…" Such a display of resolve and fortitude in the face of loss and death!

A clergyman also impacted me in a powerful way when he came for prayer after 9/11. He told me that he had always had a short fuse and tended to blow up at the slightest provocation. He shared that on 9/11 he had been running late for a flight out of Boston. As he ran through the terminal to his gate, he saw the ground crew shut the jet way door. Arriving at the gate totally flustered, he not-so-calmly asked to board even though the door was closed. He was firmly told no. He pitched a fit. He was very angry and upset to be refused when he could see his plane sitting right there in front of him! Later, while he was trying to book another flight, the news broke that a plane had hit the World Trade Center. It was the very plane he had tried to board: American Airlines Flight 11. This revelation eventually broke him. When he came to see me, I saw in him the raw faces of collateral damage, survivor's guilt, and PTSD—all wrapped up in one broken man. As he spoke to me, he actually slid off the chair onto the floor. I shall never forget my feelings as I looked upon this devastated man on the floor, trying to cope with his grief and despair. I envisioned him pressing his face and hands upon the glass as the plane, he so desperately wanted to board, pushed back from the gate without him.

A God-incident? I have been told so very many stories

from that fatal day where people who worked in the towers or had appointments to be there, for some reason did not get to the towers on time. Their lives were spared, but they continue to pay a price because this trauma has captured their spirits. Though it has been said that time heals wounds, we heard in Rose Kennedy's own words previously, that we continue to carry those wounds. Those wounds are often bound with the very grave clothes of Lazarus. There must come a time when we decide that we no longer need to live like this. The grave clothes can be removed; unbound to set the captives free from their painful memories.

Six months after 9/11, I witnessed collateral damage in the lives of care givers. I had the privilege of praying for some of the therapists who had cared for the survivors and the families of the deceased. These dear and caring souls listened to story after story about 9/11 in their offices day after day. Then they went home to more coverage of that dreadful day on television. These therapists were burnt out and were exhibiting symptoms of PTSD themselves. The steady stream of auditory and visual trauma became too much for many of them to handle. They needed Critical Incident Debriefing (CID) themselves. Working with them and listening to them, I began to realize that they needed more of God in their lives to help them cope with their own trauma and to also help them know how to support their patients.

I learnt a lot about trauma during this time. As one who has been wounded from extreme trauma myself, I am learning how to better help those who are traumatized. There is such great wisdom in the Bible. In the Gospel of John 3:30 it says *"He must become greater; I must become less."* I've learnt that I must get out of the way of God, so He can do what He does best: heal! The next verse, 31, of John's Gospel goes on to say, *"The one who comes from above is above all; the one who is from the earth belongs to the earth, and speaks as one from the earth. The one who comes from heaven is above all."* Of course we need God to sort this all out! The things of this earth may be too much with us so that we may not know what another human needs in order to be healed. But God, the One Who comes from above, from heaven, does know and He will tell us!

In closing, might you consider praying the Prayer of St. Francis with me?

"Lord, make me an instrument of your peace: where there is hatred, let me sow love; where there is injury, pardon; where there is discord, union; where there is doubt, faith; where there is despair, hope; where there is darkness, light; where there is sadness, joy.

Grant that I may not so much seek to be consoled as to console; to be understood as to understand; to be loved as to love. For it is in giving that we receive, it is in pardoning that we are pardoned, and it is in dying that we are born to eternal life." Amen

As I carry on in this call to healing that God has given me, I pray these words to be a reality, *"Lord, make me an instrument of Your peace…"* May the healing grace of God be upon this nation as it still heals from the wounds of September 11, 2001.

CHAPTER TEN

Trauma on the Battlefield of Life: Terrorism

The tension of the unfinished business of trauma.

Aren't you the Egyptian who started a revolt
and led four thousand terrorists out into the desert
some time ago?"
Paul answered, "I am a Jew, from Tarsus in Cilicia, a
citizen of no ordinary city.
Please let me speak to the people."

Acts 21:38-39

Trauma on the battlefield of life is something we all experience in some form during our lives. There are so many sources of trauma. Just taking a quick inventory of the traumas in your own life can be traumatic! In combat, the stress of merely seeing the face of the enemy causes trauma. On the battlefield of life, the actual face of our enemy may take the form of father, mother, a neighbor, an uncle, an aunt, a brother, a sister, a friend of the family or a babysitter. Terrorism can even be present in your own home. For instance, there is the terror of a controlling husband who orders, in addition to a litany of other rules, that his wife place the salt on the left and the pepper on the right in front of his plate. After a period of time, the wife learns all his quirks and obliges him accordingly. To keep the upper hand and to continue the reign of terror over his wife, the husband may suddenly change the rules and demand, "I told you to put the salt on the right and the pepper on the left, why can't you learn woman?" This sort of mind breaking control constitutes terrorism. For the victim, it is a lose-lose situation, there can be no winning. She is broken down bit by bit by the dis-ease of control and terrorism.

Humanity must endure many -*isms*, but the '*ism*' of terror is a very nasty piece of work! Terrorism is not new. We have already seen, in the verse from Acts 21 quoted at the beginning of this chapter, that Paul was accused of leading 4,000 terrorists. In the Contemporary English Version (CEV) of the Bible, two more references are made in the Gospels of Matthew and John. Barabbas, the criminal who was set free by Pontius Pilate when the crowd demanded that Jesus be crucified, is described as a terrorist. In Matthew 27:16, Barabbas is referred to as *"a well-known terrorist"*! Terrorism comes in many forms and has a variety of names and faces. There is the terror of a maniacal or tyrannical boss, the Hitler syndrome, the hitter, the control freak, the political terrorist, the religious terrorist, the jihadist, the bully, the misogynist, the misandrist, the bigot, the cynic—the list is endless! I would describe terrorists as those wanting control over others in an effort to get their way, in whatever way it takes; using strong or foul language, violence and even the threat of death. They remind me of those neighborhood gangs that wander the streets seeking supremacy by intimidation and imposing ritualistic rules in order for others to "join the club."

Who has been a terrorist in your life? How have you been hurt by fear and intimidation? Who has bullied you? Who has wounded you? Who has or had control over you? Who has used threats and coercion to get you to do what they want you to do? I could go on and on here. The reality is that we all have suffered people and groups of people who want control over us. Perhaps you, yourself, are a controller and these words are hitting home as you recognize this trait within you? Perhaps, if you have bullied or gotten your way using these tactics, you will now examine your life and see the truth? Perhaps you'll come to understand the error of your ways and seek forgiveness and reconciliation? Can you challenge yourself to get your life right with God?

How many of us, as children, were controlled by the invisible boogieman hiding under the bed or in the closet? I am a former Green Beret Royal Marine Commando and we often trained and worked in the dark of night. Boogiemen don't bother me ... or so I thought! Only recently I realized that the boogieman was still around. I awoke one night, after a nasty dream, and found myself feeling anxious and thinking about the darkness just as I had as a kid. But unlike my childhood days, I envisioned the Lord standing by my bed and I stretched out my hand into the darkness ... in confident fear! I asked the Lord to take my hand. As soon as I asked, peace immediately fell upon me and that very old demon of fear was conquered. The boogieman took a hike and hasn't been back since! The solution was the presence of the Lord. He can take away your fears. But if you're reluctant to ask Him to get rid of your boogieman, you can always try cutting off the legs of your bed!

As an adult I have come to realize that I am never alone. The Lord is with us always. I have found this certainty very helpful in my continued journey of healing. There is an expression, "waiting for the other shoe to drop." When suffering from PTSD, there is a constant fear and anticipation of an unknown. We wait for something to happen, only to find that it never does. On patrol in Northern Ireland, I was always waiting for a round to hit me. I was always waiting for a bomb to go off. I was always waiting for the other shoe to drop!

This expression "waiting for the other shoe to drop" had its origin in apartment living. The downstairs neighbor grows to learn the habits of the upstairs neighbor as he listens to the ceiling noises above. When the downstairs neighbor hears one shoe hit the floor overhead, he waits. And he waits and waits ... for the other shoe to drop! The downstairs neighbor stays alert, waiting. Has the neighbor upstairs fallen asleep before taking off his other shoe? It's taking forever for that other shoe to fall! The void, this place of endless waiting, is one feeling I was very accustomed to for years. *This is the very tension of the unfinished business of trauma!* This dreadful waiting paralyzes us even when we know that there is no actual threat, no sniper, no planted bomb, and no boogieman hiding under the bed or in the closet. Though we realize that there is no physical threat present, here's the rub: our mind still thinks there is! This void, this waiting for 'something' to happen, can remain with us for many years after the original trauma. This is the terrorism of living with PTSD.

The endless waiting for 'something' to happen is a very familiar and often unspoken feeling common among those who suffer from PTSD. Anxiety builds up and butterflies within get very busy as they morph into a swarm of angry bees defending their hive. Tension mounts within until it is broken by a loud voice or a violent startle response. Such "over reaction" to minor disturbances can result in an outburst of emotion, often anger. Companions, or simply others who happen to be around at the time, become extremely uncomfortable. They wait. They, too, wait "for the other shoe to drop." When I pray for the friends and families of PTSD victims, I often hear sentiments like this, "I feel as though I'm treading on egg shells when I'm around him." After the trauma, another battle begins: the battle for sanity.

This phenomenon induces terror in the lives of everyone around. If the PTSD victim does not receive help, it can destroy important relationships. A major obstacle is that the victim finds it very hard to ask for help. A spouse, or other person close to the victim, who might suggest that the victim seek help will be "told off." The victim often feels that to ask for help is an admission of guilt. A man with PTSD may even perceive an offer to get help as an affront to his manhood. "I can cope with this whatever it takes." In the process, primary and important relationships are threatened as the distance widens between victims and their loved ones. PTSD sufferers are very wounded souls subjected to the terrorizing wiles of their unhealed traumatized minds. They suffer a void or vacuum where they internalize a never-ending suspense of "waiting for the other shoe to drop."

My purpose in writing this book is that you will come to know that healing is available, that rifts in relationships can be healed, that your 'war on terror" can be won! *This is the very tension of the unfinished business of trauma.*

Adult children of alcoholic/drug-abuser parents or adult parents and siblings of alcoholic/drug-abuser children are also survivors and experience terrorism. These survivors are also well acquainted with the phenomenon of waiting for "something" to happen. Lying awake at night, waiting in fear for the sound of the key in the front door. Listening for the familiar sound of creaking stairs as they anxiously await the confrontation. Will it be an onslaught of mere verbal abuse or something more menacing this time? Alcoholics and drug-abusers are "in-house" terrorists. They cause long term stress and emotional disabilities. I hear stories of the enormous terror felt by their survivors who often have never told anyone before. When these survivors finally tell their stories, they sound more like confessions of *their* sin; when in reality their stories recount the diabolic sin of their perpetrators—the alcoholic or drug abuser.

These terrorists may not look any different from just regular persons. But as they consume substances that unleash evil within them, they terrorize the lives of those who live with them. When they're "not under the influence", their harmless demeanor reminds me of a suicide bomber wearing an overcoat to conceal an explosive with a very short fuse. Very often outsiders find it difficult to believe these terrorists are capable of doing any harm. When sober they can be charming, affable and fun loving. So how do their loved ones survive? Well, I've actually had some survivors tell me that they took up smoking in the hope that second hand smoke would kill their in-house terrorists. The constant stress from living in this dysfunction has enormous consequences and often warps the thinking of the survivors. When I consider the axiom of "dysfunctional family," I immediately think of the effect of alcohol and drugs where every member of a family is afflicted.

I was privileged to go to a preparatory boarding school in the UK. It was very expensive for my parents and, sadly, I was not happy there at all. I was the victim of terrorists, more commonly called school bullies. Several of these bullies caused me to live in constant threat. I wrote a letter to my parents asking that they get me out of that place. They did come for me and they actually rescued me—right out of a math class! I had been totally demoralized while there. I'm grateful and fully understand why that school is now closed. The Headmaster's discipline consisted of six whips of a bamboo cane for serious offenders. The welts would often bleed. I narrowly escaped his cane when I was once threatened with it for trying to defend myself against the bullies. I got in trouble even though I was not at fault. I left that school and went to a local school. I encountered another problem at the new school because I stood out. I was viewed as being well dressed and since I spoke the "Queen's English," I was not well received by the locals! I got bullied again! As I think back on this, I wonder whether I joined the Marines just so I could learn to defend myself? Not so bad since it really has worked. I haven't been bullied since!

I recall being concerned later in life for a younger friend. Before he headed off for a new school I taught him some self-defense moves I had learnt from my Marine training. Now I hope it wasn't because of my concern, but just as I expected, on the first day of school my friend encountered a school terrorist who was trying to bully him. My friend, having been forewarned, wanted nothing to do with this kind of terrorism. So after taking a bit of this abuse, he took charge of the situation ... if you know what I mean. He used the moves I had taught him and put that bully out of commission! My friend became the school hero and no one ever messed with him again! Try as I might not to gloat about this, I still feel a sense of redemption. Knowing that my friend took out his bully, I felt like I had won a victory over mine as well! Of course, we can't condone the use of force as the way to deal with bullies. Isn't that rather like doing the very thing you don't want done to you? But I confess, the story of my friend's triumph felt very good to me at the time!

Sadly I have heard and seen evidence of terrorism in the workplace. Do school bullies just grow up to become workplace bullies when they get bigger? It is a growing problem. I have listened to many stories and prayed for many victims of workplace terrorism. The "grown-up" playground bullies still practicing their craft. It is just so pitiful. We've all witnessed this on the highway when another driver moves to the middle of the road, challenging others to move over. Untreated, this despicable behavior escalates and so does its impact upon others. For these terrorists, it can be a lifetime scenario as old habits refuse to die. They resemble animals striving for dominance by intimidating others. Instances of sexual harassment, short fuses, thin skin, inappropriate interactions, sabotage, favoritism, discrimination, sexism, ageism, alcoholism, drug abuse, slander, theft, etc., are just some of the ploys of workplace bullies. But all is not lost for bullies. I have met many self-confessed bullies who, as adults, came to understand their error. Many became Christians and with God's help overcame their former behaviors. I am even aware of some former bullies who have attended their high school reunions and asked their former victims for forgiveness. Thank God, they have been able to let go of their need to "lord it" over others.

As a former Drill Instructor, I thought I was a tough guy! I thought I had seen it all. But several years ago, I ran into three unrepentant terrorists who opened my eyes to the devious evil peculiar to this particular form of terrorism. For twenty years, I have heard thousands of formal confessions in the process of helping others heal. In their confessions, people are able to move into a new place of peace and understanding. But these three unrepentant sinners that I encountered, endeavored to deceive me and had no intention of repenting or changing their behavior. In fact, these three pedophiles relished their continued power and control over much younger and weaker people. Perhaps I was naïve, wanting to see them come out of their darkness, but I can tell you I was shocked at their brazen and evil modus operandi. These characters zeroed in on youth in churches. When I realized that they were trying to use me to get to the youth, my 'bully radar" was activated.

I was so shocked and angered. They tried to manipulate the Christian belief that we are all sinners and that the church welcomes sinners with the intention of helping them to turn from their wicked ways. But these deviant characters had no intention of turning anywhere but toward doing further evil. They tried to prey upon the compassion of the church as a way to score future victims for their deviant desires.

With God's help as I worked with them, I began to discern Christ's truth in this situation. In the end, these three deviants were banned from ever setting foot on our premises again. After dealing with them, I actually went to the bathroom and vomited. Terrorists such as these three are the very dregs of society. They are unreachable, impenetrable and, by their choice, remain untouchable. With God's help, in earnest, I try not to judge individuals who I encounter in ministry, but I have to confess that I did judge the actions of these individuals. An unrepentant sinner chooses to remain in utter darkness and displays sickness in its most vile form.

Jesus referred to Himself as the Light. Here is what the Gospel of John 3:19-20 says about the Light, *"This is the verdict: Light has come into the world, but men loved darkness instead of light because their deeds were evil. Everyone who does evil hates the light, and will not come into the light for fear that his deeds will be exposed."* I take such comfort in these words of St. John. God is so faithful, that while I was at risk of being deceived by these three characters, the Light of the world shined upon their darkness and exposed their evil deeds to me. The Lord is so faithful that we can rest in the knowledge that He will reveal the motivations of terrorists even when they attempt to disguise themselves. If you have suffered at the hands of terrorism, there is healing available, I can say that with complete confidence. And if, in reading this chapter, you have recognized your own acts of terrorism, my prayer is that you will take this opportunity to repent and turn away from your evil deeds and come into the Light, Jesus Christ, Who is willing and able to forgive you and lead you in the paths of His righteousness. St. Paul wrote in Romans 13:12, *"The night is nearly over; the day is almost here. So let us put aside the deeds of darkness and put on the armor of light."*

As I have said throughout this chapter, there are many faces of terrorism and often that face is disguised in the same way a mask is worn. With God's help you can discard your mask. With God's help you can be set free to live your life fully. In Christ's words to the woman caught in the act of adultery, *"Go now and leave your life of sin."* (John 8:11)

CHAPTER ELEVEN

Clinical Issues, By-Products of PTSD.

I don't drink anymore,
But I don't drink any less either!
Anonymous

"and the master of the banquet tasted the water that had been
turned into wine. He did not realize where it had come from,
though the servants who had drawn the water knew. Then he
called the bridegroom aside and said, "Everyone brings out the
choice wine first and then the cheaper wine after the guests have
had too much to drink; but you have saved the best till now."
This, the first of his miraculous signs, Jesus performed in Cana
of Galilee. He thus revealed his glory, and his disciples put their
faith in him."

John 2:9-11

Sadly, a by-product of PTSD is self-medication, a coping
mechanism for the coping mechanism! *"Self-medication*
is use of a drug with therapeutic intent but without professional
advice or prescription. There are legal constraints on self-
medication, however: it may overlap with recreational drug
use, and there is a psychiatric model in which abuse is seen as
a form of self-medication. Some drugs, including aspirin and
paracetamol, are licensed for sale for self-medication, and
licensed manufacturers (pharmaceutical companies) combine
them with other substances to create a wide range of branded
products sold over the counter. Also, legal use may be made
of drugs such as alcohol and tobacco which are not covered by

drug control laws. Possession of prescription-only drugs for self-medication may be legal, but such drugs are not legally supplied for this purpose…As different drugs have different effects, they may be used for different reasons. According to the self-medication hypothesis (SMH), the individuals' choice of a particular drug is not accidental or coincidental, but instead, a result of the individuals' psychological condition, as the drug of choice provides relief to the user specific to his or her condition. Specifically, addiction is hypothesized to function as a compensatory means to modulate affects and treat distressful psychological states, whereby individuals choose the drug that will most appropriately manage their specific type of psychiatric distress and help them achieve emotional stability."[8]

Many PTSD sufferers turn to a drug of choice to help mask or cover their symptoms. They need help simply to cope with the daily task of emotional survival. These include but are not limited to: smoking, alcohol, drugs, and other mind altering substances obtained over the counter or illegally. These substances become a crutch to temporarily relieve the sufferer. They often interfere with the process of healing by creating more mental and physical problems than they resolve. Drugs of choice may mask symptoms of PTSD in the short term but in their long term use, they only compound the suffering.

"Heaping coal upon coal" they cause damage to other parts of the body. Trying desperately to win the battle for their sanity, victims defend themselves against incoming attacks on their mental stability by taking cover behind these drugs.

---

[8] http://www.essaydepot.com/doc/24107/Sef-Medication-Is-Harmful)

Chain smoking, the constant need for nicotine is a major drug of choice for use in calming the nerves and the mind. My best friend, Lt. Col. William Quayle, of the British Artillery died a horrible death following thirty eight years of smoking. He told me that he wanted people to know this, "Please don't smoke. It will eventually kill you." Will had to drink liquid morphine in order to swallow as the cancer affected his throat and esophagus. His lungs were full of black tar. Since my own run-in with H1N1, my lungs are only functioning at sixty five percent. I can spot a smoker at ten paces! My lungs actually react and I start to cough as I near cigarette smoke! My dear grandfather, Duncan McCowen, gave me a cigarette when I was about thirteen years old. I didn't let him see me throw up afterwards! Luckily I did not get addicted to tobacco, except for using a pipe for a while and an occasional cigar every now and then. Today my lungs are so damaged from H1N1 that I can't handle even the smell of a cigarette!

I have, many times, prayed with people who desire to stop smoking. With the supplicants' permission I anoint their heads, all around, declaring to each, "Jesus wore a crown of thorns, will you wear a crown of Crosses?" I anoint them praying that the mental and physical desires for nicotine will be broken. I also anoint the two fingers of their left or right hands, the very fingers that hold the cigarettes. Then I place my index finger between their fingers as if it were a cigarette and I squeeze down on those fingers. My hope is that this will make a lasting impression on the fingers which formerly found such comfort holding that instrument of death. This physical squeezing helps connect the brain to the fingers, giving them a substantial and obvious re-direct. I have found over the years that this prayer has helped many people turn away from the desire and familiar comfort of nicotine.

There was an eighty-six-year-old woman who once interrupted a Sunday sermon when she walked up the aisle right in the middle of my homily. We preachers don't really like that too much! I asked her how I could help. She turned to the congregation and told them that she had been smoking since she was thirteen and now wanted to stop. I accompanied her to the altar where she crushed her pack of cigarettes and surrendered her lighter there. She gave me a smile and then sat back down in her pew. I tried to pick up the homily where I had left off!

Two weeks later, I noticed eighteen people sitting together in tight formation at the back of the church during service. The eldest son in this gang of eighteen stood up later during testimony time and said, "Nigel, my mother has been smoking for seventy-three years. She came here two weeks ago and after you prayed for her, she has not had a cigarette since. If this great-great-grandmother can stop smoking, there must be a God! Because of her healing, all of us would like to have Christ in our lives!" Well, that was a show stopper. I had the family come up to the altar and we prayed a prayer of salvation over the whole lot of them. Such an act of faith! After the prayer, the congregation gave them a standing ovation. It was all very moving. A lifelong desire for nicotine can be cured. The smoker can be set free!

Another form of self-medication familiar to those struggling with PTSD, is overeating; an addiction to food. Many women, who were either raped or sexually abused in the past, have confessed that they overeat in order to increase their size in the hope of repelling male advances. This admission almost always comes with much sobbing and shame but, as they allow themselves to speak freely, the truth begins to set them free. As the truth settles in, these dear souls learn that they've willingly stressed their hearts and lungs and suffered other health issues of obesity; all in order to defend themselves against future incidents of rape or abuse. What enormous healing comes when they realize that there is a gentler, more constructive way to cope with their trauma.

If you struggle with overeating, let me offer this practical suggestion that may help you: try putting a Bible near your refrigerator and place another in a zip-lock bag inside the fridge. Whenever you feel like "grazing" or opening the fridge for a snack, open the Bible by the fridge first. Feast on the Word of God! Try playing Bible roulette and see what verse comes up. If you still can't resist, go ahead and open the refrigerator and take out that Bible in the zip-lock bag. Once again open up the good book and see what the Lord wants you to read. Find out what He has for you to feast on. After going through those two roadblocks, having feasted on the Word of God, ask yourself if you "need" that snack. I also recommend putting a Bible in the glove compartment of your car so you can feast on the Word while waiting in line at a drive-thru. As your car gets closer and closer to the microphone, you may be able to say to the one taking orders, "Sorry, I've changed my mind." Go on. Give it a shot.

Alcohol is another drug of choice and is frequently used to self-medicate by war torn victims. Interestingly, many states require the sale of alcohol be done only in state run stores. Often the laws of those states actually refer to alcohol as "spirits"! Drowning ourselves in alcohol, blocks God's Holy Spirit while putting out a welcome mat for a host of other not-so-desirable spirits. Drinking only temporarily hides the issues. It is never long before there's need for further hiding which leads right back to drinking again. Alcohol fogs the mind. We hide behind the bottle as if it were a concrete bunker giving us protection from an enemy sniper. Alcoholism is a very real threat to the lives of those living with PTSD. Few alcoholics can bring themselves to admit that they are prisoners to drink. Bill W. and Dr. Bob, founders of Alcoholics Anonymous, should be sainted. Their protocol for recovery has helped countless millions be rescued from death. If you or a loved one is self-medicating with alcohol, there are a lot of resources out there to help restore your sanity.

I met a Baptist couple, professional singers many years ago. They had been involved in a horrific car accident after a singing at a wedding. The husband had sustained a traumatic brain injury (TBI) which left him at a functional age of eight years old. His wife was his constant caregiver. The couple had not been drinking nor was alcohol served at the wedding where they had performed. The facility where the wedding was held did have alcohol on its premises— locked behind a metal screen. But because alcohol was on the premises their pastor condemned them and told them that their accident was a result of alcohol. What a horrible thing to say! When the wife came for healing prayer, she was totally broken. I reminded her that the judgment of the pastor was cruel and unnecessary and had contributed to her diagnosis of PTSD after the accident. Rigid religiosity and harsh judgment had reared their ugly heads. I also reminded her of Jesus' first miracle when He turned water into wine at a wedding (John 2:9-11). She was most relieved as she felt condemnation and judgment lifted off their shoulders. The peace of the Holy Spirit came upon both husband and wife as healing took place.

I had a dear friend by the name of the Rev. Dr. Harold "Hap" Carrier. Hap had been a professor at a prestigious university before he was ordained. As a priest he was very public about his past drinking and his alcohol addiction. He often spoke of the moment he knew he had crossed the line. The moment he knew he had reached bottom and made the decision to get help. Hap had been drinking all afternoon and had run out of alcohol. He staggered to the back of his house where he remembered throwing away a bottle of liquor in the garbage. He found himself in his suit, lying on the ground, rummaging through the trash can desperately trying to find that bottle. When he finally found it, he sucked the last drop out of the bottom of that bottle. It was then that he had a revelation. He had bottomed out. He had come to a place of deprivation and panic. Here was a wise professor lying amongst the trash, desperate for more booze. That was the moment when he made the decision to get help to stop drinking. He later became the president of the Troy, NY chapter of Alcoholics Anonymous. For the rest of his life until his death from cancer, Hap saved many lives in his crusade to help people turn away from alcohol, one day at a time. I learned a lot from Hap. I miss my old friend, my pal.

Perhaps the most ineffective way of fleeing trauma is the sad choice so many are taking today, during and after combat duty. Of course, I am referring to the final decision: suicide. Sadly my former brother-in-law made that decision and I witnessed the total destruction that his decision left behind. Brokenness, utter despair, raw pain and guilt are what suicide leaves in its wake for those who remain. Loved ones and friends are left with questions they cannot find answers to, "What should I have done?" "What if I had only?" "Why didn't he talk to me?" "How could I have been so blind?" Extreme sadness and despair is felt by survivors after a person takes his or her own life. Suicide is a deadly permanent solution to a temporary problem. Unfortunately at this writing it is endemic as young men and women, having witnessed man's inhumanity to man during raw combat, decide to quit trying to cope with their pain.

Living with extreme PTSD can create hopelessness in its victims, but a decision to end life does not make pain stop; it just spreads the pain around to all who ever loved or cared for the one who dies. With God's help all things are possible. There is help. Suicide is not an option and it is certainly not God's way to help. If you or someone you know is thinking about suicide please get help right away. Yes, we all have free will to do what we want, but suicide is not a form of "healing." Life is precious, it is a gift. The One Who made you and called you by your name at the moment of your birth is with you now. If you cry out to Him and call upon His name, He will answer you. Psalm 72:12-13 says, *"For He will deliver the needy who cry out, the afflicted who have no one to help. He will take pity on the weak and the needy and save the needy from death."* Perhaps you might try reading the following verse aloud, putting your own name where I have put mine in Psalm 91:14-16, *"Because* **Nigel** *loves Me,"* says the LORD, *"I will rescue* **him***; I will protect* **Nigel***, for* **he** *acknowledges My name.* **Nigel** *will call upon Me, and I will answer* **him***; I will be with* **Nigel** *in trouble, I will deliver* **him** *and honor* **him***. With long life will I satisfy* **Nigel** *and show* **him** *My salvation."*

With God's help addictions can be cured. With Him in your life you will find you no longer have need to self-medicate. Bring the Lord into all the facets of your life, inviting Him to help. This option is the most powerful way to live and the only way to overcome the daily temptations of straying like lost sheep. I have heard that it takes only twenty-one days to break a habit. This is Day One for you! If you have a destructive habit, seek help immediately. Be proactive. There are people who can help you, Godly men and women who have been called to the ministry of helping free people from addictions. People much like my old pal, Hap.

The disciples put their faith in Christ after they witnessed the water being turned into wine. It was at that moment they knew, that they knew. How about you?

Chapter Twelve

The Trigger

"The priest shall then take some of the log of oil, pour it in the palm of his own left hand, dip his right forefinger into the oil in his palm, and with his finger sprinkle some of it before the LORD seven times. The priest is to put some of the oil remaining in his palm on the lobe of the right ear of the one to be cleansed, on the thumb of his right hand and on the big toe of his right foot, on top of the blood of the guilt offering. The rest of the oil in his palm the priest shall put on the head of the one to be cleansed and make atonement for him before the LORD."

Leviticus 14:15-18

Trigger (firearms): *A mechanism that actuates the firing sequence of firearms.*[9]

Trauma trigger: *A trauma trigger is an experience that triggers a traumatic memory in someone who has experienced trauma. A trigger is thus a troubling reminder of a traumatic event, although the trigger itself need not be frightening or traumatic."* [10]

For the one who has PTSD, something, someone or some incident can trigger a traumatic memory. The back-firing of a car engine can cause a PTSD victim to hit the

---

[9] Wikipedia. (http://en.wikipedia.org/wiki/Trigger_(firearms).

[10] Wikipedia. (http://en.wikipedia.org/wiki/Trauma_trigger)

ground and roll over in self-defense.[11] A movie, a television show, a smell, a tap on the shoulder from behind, an accent, a uniform, a ringing bell, any sudden action, a group of people walking towards the victim, an anniversary, a grave marker; the list of potential triggers is endless. Triggers often initiate a series of events, when if reacted to in public, can be humiliating for the sufferer. If triggered at work, the sufferer could find his position terminated. If triggered at home, the sufferer may experience a backlash of anger, directed internally or externally. In either instance, the one struggling with PTSD will feel self-condemnation and enormous remorse. Victims recognize that they react differently to stimuli than others do. They realize that for every action, they experience an exaggerated reaction. Even their "startle responses" are vastly overstated when compared to others.

When these reactions occur in public they are deeply embarrassing to the PTSD victim, as well as to their loved ones. Frequent public displays can cause them to retreat to the safety and privacy of their own homes. A chain reaction may begin as they shy away from the company of others. In extreme cases, victims close down by isolating from family and friends. Men may find themselves spending more and more time in their "man cave" where they can hide and avoid being triggered again. Emerging from a cave can be a slow and laborious process as the sufferer tries to resume a steady pace of life. And if the victim won't re-emerge, he or she may descend into a hermit-like existence as they run away from life. They may wonder, "Is the enemy winning the battle?"

---

[11] See *Hand to Hand: From Combat to Healing*

For those who suffer exaggerated reactions to triggers, the stigma of not being able to predict or control their behaviors can cause them to spiral into depression, self-loathing, remorse, and a plethora of other emotions. Their coping mechanisms include self-medication and even driving off into the sunset for a few days to slow the pace of their triggered fly wheels. But these coping mechanisms traumatize their loved ones and cause more suffering for not only themselves but also for those who love them. The ripple effect of triggered trauma reactions is devastating.

After years of counseling others, I have found that very often our loved ones can be the trigger or push the buttons. There is a wonderful saying, "Of course your family pushes your buttons. They installed them!" I still stutter a bit when I am very stressed. The only person who sees that is my wife. As I shared earlier, for many years I was so embarrassed about it. But when I finally talked to Lynn about it, I discovered that she actually liked it and found it endearing! Having learned that she is more accepting of my stuttering than I am, helped diminish my harsh judgment of myself. Her acceptance of me helped me to become less frustrated with myself. Eventually my wife's reaction to my triggered stuttering reaction turned into a positive action and has led to a noticeable reduction in my stutter reaction! Her positive response was like a reverse trigger for me! This was a big turning point in my healing and shows how essential loved ones can be in helping PTSD victims overcome their triggers. I can signpost that conversation with my wife. It was a giant leap forward in my healing journey.

It took me years before I was able to talk about these things. But after finally getting it all off my chest, the power of those negative emotions was discharged and put in proper perspective. When sufferers are able to drag this stuff out of the darkness and bring it into the light, they see that what they thought was an elephant, was really just an ant. The triggers get smaller as healing slowly takes place. Becoming transparent in the healing process means becoming vulnerable. My identity as a tough Green Beret Special Forces Marine and all my bravado and arrogance, could not cover the wounds of my heart after such traumas. There just comes a point in our lives when, no matter how macho we are, we have to deal with these triggers. Individual trauma triggers, whatever they may be, can set the mind's flywheel off into a flashback or abreaction, carrying the PTSD sufferer back in time, reliving the memory and triggering all its actions and reactions. Feeling hot, cold, sweaty; beginning to shake and tremble to the point of shutting their minds and bodies down, are a few of the sensations felt by victims following a surge of raw response during an abreaction. This business of the unfinished business of trauma has to be dealt with before healing can take place. There comes a time when things just need to be put right.

In the process of healing the mind, we try not to pry—we pray! Trauma triggers need to be identified, spoken about, unpacked and presented. It can be a slow and extremely painful business, but it needs to be done. We simply can't just sweep it under the carpet, as much as we might want to. Present medical protocol doesn't provide for memories to be erased. Though I feel sure that one day this will happen, for now these issues must be approached in a safe and monitored way by nurturing victims and loving them "back home." I'm still working on several trauma induced reactions in my own life. When I take my wife to a restaurant there's never a conversation about where we'll be seated! It is just understood between us that I must sit facing the door: the place of threat. In addition, when possible, no one can be seated behind me! Maybe one day this habit of mine will be broken, but at the moment, I still deal with it in a way that guarantees safety. Being British, I know something of the old days of "yore." It was considered protocol that a knight would always face the door, with his sword ready. Glass always lined the bottoms of pewter tankards so that drinkers could see the "press gang" entering the pub or perhaps even see a fist coming at the face! As a Brit, I like to think that I have inherited this legacy of self-protection …Well, that's my excuse anyway!

Another trauma induced reaction that I continue to deal with, has to do with night vision. Whenever I am confronted with a strong light in the dark of night, I always close my left eye and keep my right eye open. Since I am left-handed, this reaction serves to save the night vision of my rifle eye. This can happen whether I am driving or even going to the bathroom at night. I am sitting here smiling and realizing that I have done this since 1972 it is now 2011. This is a thirty-nine year old habit that may well have saved my life in combat, but is now just an unnecessary habit. Closing my left eye like that keeps me linked to the years when I was on night patrol. I have found yet another trigger! It is as though I need to say to myself, "Nigel, the patrol has ended." I have remained on permanent patrol and I don't have to stay this way. This kind of hyper-vigilance is no longer necessary. I likely need to sit myself down and give permission, to the part of my brain that has continued this old habit, to be set free! This is actually one of the keys to healing! Jesus says in the Gospel of Luke 4:18b-19, *"He has sent me to proclaim freedom for the prisoners and recovery of sight for the blind, to release the oppressed, to proclaim the year of the Lord's favor."* I feel that my self-imprisonment, my self-imposed night blindness, can now be released. It's time for me to enjoy the year of the Lord's favor. Perhaps finally telling others about this peculiar habit is the Lord's favor and provision to break me of it. Though this may seem to be a very minor issue, it is indeed a trauma trigger; one that I've been reacting to for decades! I am very grateful to let go of some more of the unfinished business of trauma.

In the ministry of healing, I have found that the single act of anointing has enormous power. During the first Welcome Home Initiative (WHI), we gathered on the third day to pray. Whenever I pray for others, I anoint them with holy oil, in accordance with James 5:14, *"Is any one of you sick? He should call the elders of the church to pray over him and anoint him with oil in the name of the Lord."* The forehead of a supplicant is the usual place I anoint with oil. When the first veteran came forward for prayer on that first retreat, I had a huge revelation. It was as if God nudged me and gently persuaded me to ask, "Do I need to anoint your trigger finger?" He looked at me and knew what I meant immediately. We had unspoken communication—a glance of deep understanding and mutual respect, a knowing between those who have been in combat. Tears started streaming down both our faces. Slowly he raised his right hand with only his forefinger extended. His other fingers and thumb closed as he pointed his forefinger at an unseen enemy. Then the forefinger curled, symbolically pulling the trigger again! By then, he was sobbing and so were the rest of us! It was as if his finger had twitched by itself; as though that finger was saying, "Please set me free from this torment."

As I write this, however, I can now see something that escaped me then. When this veteran came forward for prayer, he had held his forearm as though it was in a sling across his chest. His forefinger was pointed across his chest to the left. And when his trigger finger twitched, as it might in reaction to a trauma memory, it caused the point of that curled finger to be aimed at his own heart! Thinking back now, it was as though the Lord was Himself supporting that man's arm, cradling it close to his chest. His trigger finger, once used to kill enemies, was now curled and pointed toward his own wounded heart! I realize now that it was *not* his finger that seemed to say, "Please set me free from this torment"; it was the cry of that soldier's wounded heart! This healing experience has become even more poignant than I remembered. It is a reminder that there is a time for everything, and a season for every activity under heaven. Ecclesiastes 3:3 tells us that there is, *"a time to kill and a time to heal, a time to tear down and a time to build."* The first WHI was a time to break down, to build up and to let go for this man's wounded heart. Triggers must necessarily be pulled in combat, but later in life those who pulled them, often experience a buildup of self-doubt and self-condemnation. This veteran was finally able to let go at that retreat. He was able to experience the comforting words of Romans 8:1, *"Therefore, there is now no condemnation for those who are in Christ Jesus."*

The act of confession and reconciliation meets our human need to be heard, understood and forgiven. And the sooner we do it, the better! Healing comes faster when it is sought closer to the time of the actual trauma. As we continued to pray at that first WHI, I made it a point of asking each combatant the same question about their trigger finger. Many offered their hands with their arms in that same sling position. We had two veterans who presented the palms of their hands. Once again, I understood this unspoken gesture as communication that they had used their bare hands in combat! One man presented his thumb for prayer. Why? That confused me. When I asked why his thumb, he told me that his thumb was the trigger to release bombs, thousands of pounds of bombs. I can tell you that after this healing session, we were all totally done in. I went off by myself to process what had happened. I just needed to be alone, though I didn't know where to go. Then it hit me that the New Testament tells of the many times Jesus went off by Himself. In God's economy, we need not reinvent anything!

I have found that whether at WHI retreats or other times when I pray, there is an anointed healing grace in the mere action of providing a time of release for those suffering buried wounds. Actions speak louder than words. In praying with combat veterans, I find that words are often unnecessary. The silent bond of warrior to warrior is comforting in itself. The knowing and understanding between fellow veterans brings peace. In such anointed moments, we find what is expressed in Philippians 4:7, *"And the peace of God, which transcends all understanding, will guard your hearts and your minds in Christ Jesus."* WHI retreats or whenever healing is available, can be the starting place for those seeking genuine peace in their lives.

Memories of trauma grow just as a boil grows. Pressure builds up and it becomes more toxic. Lancing a boil is a painful process. What is found inside is quite raw: pink, or yellow and green if it is infected. But after a boil is lanced, air can then get to it. What was toxic is removed and what remains is cleansed. The skin can now heal. Rehashing the past is like lancing a boil. As the wound is exposed to the light, what was toxic in the memory is removed and what remains is cleansed. Though it hurts, the memory of the trauma can heal. Triggers can be disarmed and redeemed.

My prayer for you is that with help you will discover your trauma triggers, whatever they are or whatever they represent. May those triggers be presented in a safe place. May the boils be lanced, the toxins released and the wound healed. May you be set free from the captivity of your trauma memories. May you know true peace.

CHAPTER THIRTEEN

Telling Your Story

"Do two people walk hand in hand if they
aren't going to the same place?
Does a lion roar in the forest if there's
no carcass to devour?
Does a young lion growl with pleasure
if he hasn't caught his supper?
Does a bird fall to the ground
if it hasn't been hit with a stone?
Does a trap spring shut if nothing trips it? When the
alarm goes off in the city, aren't people alarmed? And
when disaster strikes the city, doesn't God stand behind
it? The fact is, God, the Master, does nothing without
first telling his prophets the whole story."

Amos 3:3-7 (The Message)

Reckless words pierce like a sword,
but the tongue of the wise brings healing.

Proverbs 12:18

"Christians don't always see eye to eye
but they can always walk arm in arm!"

J. John

Since 1990 I have had the privilege of listening to the stories of people in a healing setting. I try to listen, love and pray. I listen to what people are saying and to what they are not saying. At the same time, I try to listen to what God is saying. I love people and I pray with all my heart, mind, body and soul. The Old Testament prophet, Amos, wrote that God does nothing without first telling his prophets the whole story. Without the whole story we do not have the complete picture. I have heard so many stories. Some are tame while other stories are so horrendous that I cannot recount them here without possibly traumatizing you and, frankly, re-traumatizing myself! It is an amazing blessing and a divine experience to hear the confessions of people who have suffered trauma and carry tremendous burdens. During those sacred moments I serve as Christ's ambassador, a trustworthy silent companion, while the confessor addresses the Lord directly. *"We are therefore Christ's ambassadors, as though God were making his appeal through us. We implore you on Christ's behalf: Be reconciled to God."* 2 Corinthians 5:20.

In telling your story in the presence of those who listen, love and pray, you are being reconciled to yourself and to God as He brings you to acceptance. God adjusts, settles and sorts out the unfinished business of your trauma. Perfect friends are good listeners, they may even put their hands over their mouths to keep from talking, so as not to interrupt you. They pay attention to every detail and really listen to what you're saying, only interrupting to clarify a thought, but never to compare scars! To really listen to others is a gift to humanity, as so many people have much to say and few listen. A good listener has a true gift of understanding and compassion. This is what is meant when we *"put on the mind of Christ."* 1 Corinthians 2:16b

There was a well-known psychiatrist on Harley Street in London who had a very busy private practice. Though he was very expensive, a man with little income went to see him with a proposition. "Look" the man said, "I know you're busy and I'm not able to pay your full price, but would you consider allowing me to tell my story to you as you eat lunch in your office?" The doctor agreed, reduced his rates considerably, and ate his sandwich as he listened to the man. The doctor simply spoke a few words to the man during each session. In several months, the man got himself sorted out! That man was very creative in getting his needs met. His story reminds me of the persistent widow in the Gospel of Luke 18:1-8. Like the widow, this man's persistence and perseverance paid off. He found his healing!

Recently a woman came for prayer. When she told me her story, I was shocked. It sounded like something out of a horror movie. What a persecuted life of terror! After she finished sharing, I tried my usual way of trying to unpack her story, seeking clarification. But in her case, nothing came to my mind. We sat in silence for a while, as I prayed like crazy. "Oh Lord! I don't know what to say." More silence. I knew then that I must simply confess to her what was going on. For the first time in twenty years, I did not know what I was to say. So, I told her honestly, "I am so amazed at what has happened in your life, that for the first time in twenty years, I do not know what to say." I didn't feel good about saying that; in fact, I was at a complete loss and feeling totally defeated. What do you say to someone who has had such an awful life? She looked me right in the eye, smiled and sweetly said, "That's okay, I just needed someone to understand and validate what I've been through." I took a deep breath of relief, smiled back, and thanked God for this woman's gracious response. She needed to tell her story to someone who would listen.

More often than not, we are not listened to. Husbands do you really listen to your wives? Did you even know that the Bible says that husbands should live with their wives in an understanding way? How can you understand her if you don't listen to her? People from my past are coming to my mind right now. You probably know people just like them. I might say, "I feel achy all over today," and they respond, "Me too! I think I'm coming down with the flu." Or I say, "I have such a headache," and they respond, "I get migraines, I'm having a CT scan next week." You know the type, those who have to "one up" you. Let me tell you something important: this sort of game cannot happen in the healing ministry! Comparing scars with supplicants is totally out of the question. Those who are privileged to hear your story must really listen and pay attention to your words and even to your body language. Those worthy of hearing your story will likely square off with you, making full eye contact, arms open, even leaning in toward you a little. They will be fully engaged in listening and paying close attention to you. They may also occasionally restate or confirm what has been said, reinforcing that you are being heard. If you happen to be the one who has been asked to hear someone's story, take note of what I've written here. It is a privilege to be chosen to listen to another's story. In accepting this responsibility, remember that you are holding a soul in your hand.

Personally I believe that people need to tell their story in a safe place. Most people need to be fully heard and understood. I am not suggesting that we all go around telling our horror stories until we are blue in the face. What I am suggesting is that somewhere out there is someone who is compassionate and caring and has been sent by God to help you. I see the fruit of this phenomenon every day. Traumatized people, by simply telling their stories, become empowered to overcome the negativity in their pasts. Finding that person sent by God as your safe place to invest the telling of your story will greatly reduce the power of the perpetrators of your trauma memories. They will no longer pose a real threat. It's like getting an all clear: 'The threat has left your life!'

I have witnessed the benefit of sharing stories, most effectively, in ministering to returning combatants. World War II veterans traditionally have never told their entire stories to their families or to anyone, for that matter. Even veterans returning from today's theaters of war tend not to tell their stories fully. It was remarkable to help a ninety-one year old unpack his story of Pearl Harbor and other horror stories of his combat experience. He had never told anyone of these events which occurred when he was twenty-four! His humble, kind and smiling manner and warm heart gave no inkling of the horrors stored in his mind. As he spoke, those in our group traveled back with him and peeked into a history he had never processed. What a privilege it was to see the Lord provide a safe place for this man, who in his youth had been so traumatized and had never spoken of it. He could unload all of it without fear of judgment. Now that's what I call healing! The fruit was seeing his face full of joy and an even broader smile than before. The rest of us? Well, our faces were covered in tears of joy. He looked great, but we all looked a mess. What a privilege it is to watch God heal!

In the past, the military only focused on the physical aspect of being fit for combat, or what is called combat readiness. Battle fitness tests (BFT) only assessed the physical preparedness of combatants. But now attention is also being given to spiritual fitness. I have personally observed that those who are also spiritually fit, fare better than those who are not. In and through exercising faith, veterans are more prepared to bear the burden of their combat history. I met a young, combat veteran at a healing service, who told me that he had shot a seventeen year old father of two in Iraq. He said that he shot him because the seventeen year old had just shot his friend. As I listened to this lad, I was amazed at how he told his story with confidence. As he looked me in the eye, he told me what had happened in a very matter of fact manner. It was obvious to me that he was a Christian. I could see a genuine peace in him that surprised even me as he spoke. His story will not wait until he is ninety-one. His spiritual fitness allowed him to share his story in an honest and real way soon after it occurred. He didn't try to cover up the memory of this wound. This trauma will not follow that young man to his grave. Through Christ all things are possible.

So many WWI and WWII veterans have gone to their graves without telling their stories. Today we realize that CID (Critical Incident Debriefing) is very important to the well-being of returning soldiers' minds. To be blunt, CIDs help clear out the trash. So often trauma victims are increasingly haunted by their memories. It is as though an emotional cancer is quietly growing until something snaps. The CID has the potential to help veterans process their traumas before they become buried memories. Unprocessed trauma becomes the obvious, but unmentioned elephant in the room!

Having heard thousands of stories and having helped unpack the horror, fear, grief, and pain of either real or perceived threat; it is astonishing how people are able to function even while carrying their very heavy baggage. I watch God help them unpack their bags as I listen, love and pray for them in a safe place. I am awed at His ability to make sense and restore the lives of those who have buried their memories and who have been buried by them. I have seen God unravel all the bandages in which so many are so tightly bound. I have seen Him allow a healed person to be revealed when those bandages are removed and I have prayed for myself, "Oh God, please unwrap the invisible bandages around my head and expose the healed me."

The wounded are set free from the wounds of life and

the wounding of the past when they are able to share their stories of trauma with those who are willing to listen, love and pray for them. As you walk out your journey of healing, think of how it would be to live your life without the shadow of the past hanging over you and controlling your destiny. To get started on your journey, you must see with eyes of faith that you are being set free as you learn to forgive those who wounded you. Unforgiveness will cause you more pain than your perpetrator. You need not continue to give your perpetrators ever more power over your life. It's time to walk away from the perpetrators of your pain. It's time to reach out for real power that is available only in the Lord … for He is the power and the glory, for ever and ever. Amen.

Please find yourself someone you can trust and who will listen to you. Find someone who will allow the Lord to show up and sit with you as you tell your story. Then allow that someone to help you as the Lord sorts out your past and enables you to live in the present. My prayer is that you will be set free, really free!

Chapter Fourteen

Children of the Holocaust: The Power of the Perpetrator

*"And to them will I give in my house
and within my walls a memorial and
a name (a "yad vashem")... that
shall not be cut off."*

Isaiah 56: 5

*A happy heart makes the face cheerful,
but heartache crushes the spirit.*

Proverbs 15:13

In appreciation of God's healing in her life through prayer, Betty Hanerman sent me on a trip to the Holy Land. I went there with several other pilgrims from Scotland in 1998. She gave me a gift for my soul, a trip that changed my life. I walked where Jesus walked and stood near the place Jesus had proclaimed (Luke 4:18-19), *"The Spirit of the Lord is on me, because he has anointed me to preach good news to the poor. He has sent me to proclaim freedom for the prisoners and recovery of sight for the blind, to release the oppressed, to proclaim the year of the Lord's favor."* I was privileged to read those very words to our group, in the same location where Christ Himself declared them two thousand years ago. When I finished reading, I fell to my knees in tears. I wept so much that it was difficult to breathe. I wondered, "Is this the year of the Lord's favor? Does that favor include being released from the torment of past emotional wounds? Does that favor mean freedom from memories that imprison our minds?" For me it was. I experienced a healing from shell shock in that place. At or near the spot where Jesus began his earthly ministry, He released me from the oppression of my wounded mind.

We visited many places in the Holy Land that seared my soul. I felt an emotional and spiritual overload while there, not in a bad way, but in a profound way. Later our group visited the war memorial of Yad Vashem, a place that deeply touched my heart and soul. It was established in 1953, less than a decade after the end of the concentration camps of WWII. Among its purposes are to serve as the world's repository for documentation, research, education and commemoration of the Jewish people who survived and perished in the Holocaust; to safeguard the memory of the past; and to interpret and pass on its meaning for future generations. While there I reflected on the people I had befriended as a teenager, survivors who had been in those camps.

One madman, Adolph Hitler, had convinced many to follow him on a path of destruction of the Jews. He was a contagious virus of hatred who set out to extinguish those he considered less than himself. Anti-Semitism has been around for all of history and that, of course, made Hitler's rants resonate with vast populations who cheered him on as he maniacally 'cleansed' the world. It just baffles me that one person could be so evil and hook whole nations into following him. A single madman's power was responsible for such unrestrained torture, horror and death! Just think how many others joined him in his lunacy! I am reminded of a quote from my friend, the writer Michael Kassin, who penned these lines in his play, *Peace*: "*If I killed one man I'd be a murderer. If I killed a village I'd be a butcher. If I killed six million I'd be Satan. But I made a bomb that will kill the world one day—What name is there for me? I am become death—destroyer of worlds."* Sadly, world history attests to not just one crazed 'destroyer of worlds', but to a host of madmen who preceded Hitler, as well as those who came after him; each having carried out comparable acts of cultural genocide in their own corner of the world.

As I consider the vast number of Hitler's followers, Pilate comes to mind. I imagine Pilate, a Roman governor, polling the Jerusalem crowd to determine which prisoner they preferred to have released. Their choice was between Barabbas, a murderer; and Jesus Christ, who helped and healed people. Of course we know how it turned out, the crowd shouted for Barabbas to be set free and demanded that Jesus be crucified. I can't help but wonder whether that same crowd and their mob mentality would have blindly followed Hitler. Would they have chosen evil over good, once again?

There was one building at Yad Vashem that just ripped my heart out when I visited. It is the Children's Memorial dedicated to the 1.5 million children whose lives were cut short by the Holocaust. Hollowed out from an underground cavern, this exhibition gives visitors an experience similar to those doomed children as they walked down a ramp into gas chambers, eerily disguised as showers. As I made my descent, I allowed myself to feel as though I was walking to my own death, imagining what the children must have seen and heard just prior to deadly canisters of gas being released through the overhead "showers." My thoughts considered the probability that each child must have struggled for his or her last breath as the chamber filled with lethal gases.

No sooner had my mind absorbed this assault of imagined, horrific scenes of dying children, I then became aware of what my ears had been hearing. Throughout the building, a steady stream of the names, ages and home countries of all those murdered children were being read aloud! Then I noticed, in the middle of the building, the glow of just one lighted candle. Surrounding that one candle were an infinite number of small mirrors, each with the light of that single candle reflected in them. The mirrors were arranged to repeat that reflection again and again, creating a galaxy of light. Each mirror represented the life of one child who had perished in the Holocaust. I found myself staring at that single candle for a long time and then staring at one of the mirrors and then another and another, as my mind struggled to grasp the enormity of this monstrous event in our history. Each visitor wrestled with many questions, "How could this have happened? How could mankind possibly be capable of such cruelty?"

I later learnt that it takes three full days to listen to the entire list of names that were read. The audio recording of those names is never turned off. While there, every visitor had tears running down their faces. The building was utterly silent except for the sound of those names and muffled sobs. No one spoke. What was there to say? I had stood there in awe, jaw open, staring, tears flowing freely down my cheeks. The space soon became claustrophobic for me, as I imagined it must have been for those children trapped in the "showers." I began to feel as though I couldn't breathe. I needed to get out! It had become way too much for me! And then it hit me—I could run away. I could just decide to leave. Finally a troubling thought came to me: though I had a choice to stay or leave, those helpless children had no choice.

As I write this over a dozen years later, I can better understand what was going on inside of me during this trip. I mentioned earlier that as a young lad, at the age of sixteen, I had become friends with many who had survived the concentration camps. Though I had known the particulars of what they had suffered; until this visit to Yad Vashem, my soul could not fathom what it really meant to call my friends, "survivors." Until this trip I could not conceive of what my friends had actually survived. I can still feel the pain of this awakening in me during this visit. Writing this now, I am having difficulty breathing. My tracheotomy scar feels constricted, as though I am having my throat cut all over again. I feel so much pain as I recall my friends' personal testimonies of their time in concentration camps. I can see now that I was traumatized at a young age by their stories. The palpable, agonizing response I had at Yad Vashem in 1998, was the visible residue of that trauma from my youth.

My family moved to Stagenhoe Park, an 18th century mansion near Hitchin, Hertfordshire in England. It had become a holiday home for Polish concentration camp survivors. It was operated by Sue Ryder Care, a charity named for the wife of Group Captain Lord Leonard Cheshire, VC, OM, DSO, DFC a highly decorated WWII British RAF pilot, who had been the official British observer of the bombing of Nagasaki. His future wife, Margaret Susan Ryder, had worked for the Special Operations Executive which had promoted and coordinated resistance activity in Nazi-occupied Europe. After the war, Lady Ryder opened St. Christopher's home in Germany and another in Poland to help displaced, homeless people and concentration camp survivors. When she married Baron Cheshire in 1959, they founded the Ryder-Cheshire Foundation and opened several other homes in England to alleviate suffering. Husband and wife were devoted to Christ and had converted to Catholicism. Six years after the Baron's death in 1992, the Baroness severed ties with Sue Ryder Care[12] for departing from its guidelines. In 2000, the year of her own death, the

---

[12] f/k/a Ryder-Cheshire Foundation

Baroness founded a new charity that restored the work of her husband (prior to their marriage) to help sick people get to Lourdes, France for healing!

My parents moved our family to Stagenhoe Park in the 1970s and ran that wonderful home for seven years. I can still recall a brief chat I had with Baron Cheshire when I was sixteen. Oh how I would so like to talk to him now! After the war, the Baron dedicated the rest of his life to relieve the suffering of disabled people, initially focusing on combat veterans and their families. When he married Lady Ryder, their mutual passion for caring for society's wounded became their joint mission. Though he was one of only 32 WWII RAF pilots to receive the Victoria Cross for more than one instance of heroic service, the Baron dedicated his life to peace. After the war he founded Vade in Pacem (VIP) which translates as "Go in Peace". VIP's mission was to provide a place where former WWII service personnel and their families would be assisted in transitioning to civilian life. Is it not amazing that decades later I would be used by the Lord to offer WHI, the Welcome Home Initiative, for returning veterans and their families? I am awed at how the Lord exposed me to His healing ministry at such an early age.

While at Stagenhoe Park, I met and befriended many people with tattooed numbers on their left forearms. I also met people there who were dying because of medical experiements conducted by the Nazis. Some of our "Bods" (our nickname for the residents) told me their stories that amazed and shook me to the core. How these people had suffered. Knowing their histories and then watching them laughing and dancing and eating while they were with us, had a profound impact on me. There was no mention of shell shock or PTSD. To see and meet and befriend these souls, who had been to hell and back, left a lasting impression on me. Knowing their stories, looking into their eyes, and witnessing their resilience, despite experiencing man's most vile inhumanity toward man, left no clue to one of life's great mysteries. However did these dear people get up in the morning and function? When my personal history with these concentration camp survivors was triggered at Yad Vashem, I realized just how traumatized I had been at the young age of sixteen. Looking back now, this was God teaching me about truama so I might help others in their plight today.

Jane, a dear Jewish friend of mine said to me one day, "Hitler still has power over me." This madman who died in 1945, more than sixty-five years ago, still affects her life on a daily basis. Jane lost her entire family in the Holocaust. She wonders, "Why am I alive, when all my family died?" This profound wound continues to torment Jane even though the perpetrator has been dead for decades, ruling from the grave! I recently learnt about a deceased Holocaust survivor who instructed her children to cremate her body and sprinkle her ashes at the Treblinka memorial site in Poland, so she could be reunited with her relatives who perished in that camp. This powerful grip those traumatic events and their perpetrators have on survivor's verges upon an inheritance of sorts. The wound becomes an onerous legacy that is passed on from one generation to another.

My father, an Anglican vicar in England, recently met a Polish woman whose deceased grandfather had survived the concentration camp at Auschwitz. Over coffee one day, my father learnt that her grandfather never spoke of his experiences at the camp though his left forearm and the number tattooed on it, had branded him. She told my father that throughout her life, whenever she heard the word "Auschwitz", her left forearm became extremely painful. Was this his "legacy" to her? Was this memory actually in her DNA? Certainly as a child she had been told what that number on his forearm meant and the extreme trauma that was attached to it. Henry David Thoreau is quoted as saying, *"Most men lead lives of quiet desperation and go to the grave with the song still in them."* Was the "song", now in the forearm of this woman, her grandfather's legacy?

Years ago while I was Director of the Oratory of the Little Way in Connecticut, I met two people who did not know one another but who had each made appointments to talk about healing with me on the same day—one in the morning and one later in the afternoon. They opened my eyes even further and expanded my understanding of PTSD. Both were Jewish with parents who had been interned in Nazi concentration camps. Both had been formally diagnosed with PTSD, though neither of them had themselves suffered the trauma that their parents had in those camps. They both seemed to have inherited their parents' trauma. I sat with each of them, independently, and asked, "How may I pray for you?" They both told me that they were suffering terribly. As I listened to their stories, separately, I saw that they had both taken on the burdens of that their parents' were carrying. Their eyes were even sunken like the images of those thin, broken, diminished souls in photographs taken of survivors discovered in the liberated camps at the war's end. They were walking memorials of the Holocaust. They suffered survivor's guilt, shared trauma memories and utilized many of the same coping skills to survive life in modern day New York City. It was so sad. Yet hope prevailed.

I gleaned from these two visitors that trauma can definitely become a burdensome legacy for the loved ones of trauma victims. I learnt that PTSD does not necessarily discriminate between the actual persons who experienced the trauma and those persons who "only" experienced it vicariously. It was such a privilege to pray for these broken people. Talking through what they knew deep within the very fiber of their beings and together seeking healing of their souls, was an amazing moment in my life. In both instances, I was able to witness their transformation through healing. Holding these very wounded souls in my prayers and lifting them before God to heal all the broken places, we were able to see the power of God's Word at work in their lives and how very much the Lord remains in the business of healing!

In the more than twenty years of listening, loving and praying for people, I have begun to see that though most victims have not survived concentration camps, many more have survived various other forms of madness within their own homes or in their expanded environs. Many have been subjected to comparable acts of cruelty, bullying, humiliation and condemnation as those who suffered at the hands of the Nazis. When perpetrators are not strangers, but are people who are supposed to love and care for you, the wounds can be even more devastating than those who suffered otherwise. It is heartbreaking. And yet I can see that over the span of my own life, I've been privileged to hear the stories and know the wounds of countless victims, so that I would be useful to God in His desire to heal His hurting children—no matter what their age!

Who has power over you? What memory has power over you? What is captive within you that needs to be set free?

If you are a child of any holocaust or the child of parents who served in the conflicts of war from WWI, WWII, Vietnam, Korea, Desert Storm, Iraq, Afghanistan, and all others; please take from what you have read here and seek help to heal. Let us through prayer, compassion, listening, and loving; seek ways to bring healing to the war within you. This is what the healing of PTSD is about—the healing of soul wounds. With God's help, you can remove the threat of perpetrators, render them dead and buried, proclaim the end of the war within and come into a place of peace.

In the midst of writing this chapter, I have celebrated my first anniversary of the day I nearly died whilst in a coma in 2009. Pondering this makes this chapter even more poignant for me. Though these pages have contained painful and disturbing images, I think I can wrap this chapter up with words of forgiveness. These words were written on a piece of paper found near the body of a child at Ravensbruck Concentration Camp. Let's read them together now:

> *"O Lord, remember not only the men and women of good will, but also those of ill will. But do not remember all the suffering they have inflicted; remember the fruits we have bought, thanks to this suffering—our comradeship, our loyalty, our humility, our courage, our generosity, the greatness of heart which has grown out of all of this, and when they come to judgment, let all the fruits which we have born be their forgiveness. Amen."* [13]

The sentiment of the writer of the above prayer reminds me of St. Paul's letter to the Romans 12:15-18: *"Bless those who persecute you; bless and do not curse. Rejoice with those who rejoice; mourn with those who mourn. Live in harmony with one another. Do not be proud, but be willing to associate with people of low position. Do not be conceited. Do not repay anyone evil for evil. Be careful to do what is right in the eyes of everybody. If it is possible, as far as it depends on you, live at peace with everyone."*

---

[13] Michael Counsell, compiler, 2000 Years of Prayer (Morehouse, 1999), p. 469.

Help me, O God, not to judge others, not to profile them, not to put people into categories; but give me Your heart and compassion to love You. Help me to love and forgive my neighbor as You have so commanded. Amen.

Postscript

I am sitting at my computer having just finished this chapter. My eyes are fixed on a red lantern I bought just yesterday. There is one candle in it and its light is reflected in the glass like the mirrors at the Children's Memorial at Yad Vashem. While I was in a coma for two months in 2009, I had a vision of my house in heaven. It was made of glass and red painted metal. I bought this red lantern because it reminded me of my future home. As my lantern light flickers, I am praying for all the souls who have died at the hands of others. As I look above my desk, I see His cross and I'm reminded that Jesus died that we might have life and live it abundantly. That's His promise for you! All we need do, is ask.

CHAPTER FIFTEEN

The Root of Bitterness

Do you want to get better or do you want to get bitter?
Anonymous

With bitterness archers attacked him;
they shot at him with hostility.
Genesis 49:23

"Therefore I will not keep silent; I will speak out in the
anguish of my spirit, I will complain in the bitterness
of my soul.
Job 7:11

Another man dies in bitterness of soul, never having
enjoyed anything good.
Job 21:25

The heart knows its own bitterness, and no stranger
shares its joy.
Proverbs 14:10

A serious side-effect of PTSD is bitterness. It's important to note that though bitterness is borne out of being a victim of PTSD; once victims take hold of bitterness it can energize and give momentum to the intensity of PTSD. So it becomes a vicious cycle. The experience of trauma produces PTSD. A trigger from the trauma memory sets off a severe response within victims and in the aftermath the victims' frustration, despair and guilt, bitterness is bred. Bitterness increases the intensity of responses when trauma memories are triggered within victims. This cyclical nature contributes to victims' increased embitterment and contributes to victims' decreasing control over their responses and emotions. It's a very nasty way to live! The manifestation of bitterness within PTSD victims tends to create anti-social behaviors as they isolate and build protective walls around themselves.

The Bible has many references to bitterness, none are positive and most caution against it. Sadly, it has no good purpose in our lives. It is simply not healthy for anyone. In my opinion, bitterness is a gaping soul wound that screams at others who happen to get in its path. Though there is an endless list of circumstances and experiences that can lead to bitterness, those who "own" their bitterness are like poster children that offer proof of how the enemy wins. When trauma survivors become embittered they hand over control of themselves to the perpetrators of their wounds. Becoming embittered increases the sources of triggers that set off trauma victims to act out of their pain. Bitterness saps the energy resources of PTSD sufferers and makes them feel even more powerless to cope with their wounds.

When we think of how to define bitterness, we have only to think about the simple illustration of something we have tasted. We've all experienced eating something bitter. Instantly our mouths are filled with a horrible taste that lingers unless we do something to wash it out. If we experience the bitter taste of a certain ingredient, we will naturally avoid foods that contain it in the future. Overtime we generalize about all foods that may contain that ingredient, and we avoid them. We may even warn others to stay away from it based upon our personal experience, no matter how long ago our first and only taste of it was.

Finally, without ever ingesting that ingredient again, we may respond to its scent or the mention of it, in the same way we did when we first tasted it in our mouths. We can still "taste" its bitterness in our mouths.

Well, in my experience, bitterness of the soul does something very similar to PTSD survivors. It can be all consuming and though the trauma that caused it was very painful, bitterness continues to fuel its intensity and takes control over the survivor. Bitterness in trauma victims can block healing in their lives. Not only the trauma needs healing, so does the bitterness that attached itself to the trauma. In researching this topic, I found this quote on charminghealth. com.[14] I think you will marvel as I did at this descriptive definition of bitterness; where it comes from and what it does: "**Bitterness** *is a frozen form of latent anger and resentment. Bitterness grows out of our refusal, to let go when someone or something is taken from us. Bitterness is being constantly hurt by a memory and is holding onto a hurt until it has a hold on you.* **Bitterness is the unhealthiest emotion you can have.** *When you are offended or disappointed by others and allow the hurt to germinate in your heart, bitterness and resentment will take root. Bitterness is characterized by an unforgiving spirit and generally negative, critical attitudes. Bitterness and resentment are both sinful and self-defeating.*"

As you can imagine, working with survivors of trauma as I do, I have heard many bitter people unload their grievances, rightly or wrongly, on me as they shared their stories. I frequently get an ear full of grief, sadness, injustice, raw pain and all other results of man's inhumanity to man. Whether they are victims of combat in war or of combat at home, they perceive their pain the same and are equally

---

[14] http://www.charminghealth.com/applicability/bitterness.htm

motivated toward bitterness. One very bitter man stands out for me. He certainly had just cause for his bitterness as he presented his perception of his circumstances to me, but whether his behavior was justified is another matter. I challenged him with the words that Christ answered when asked by the teachers of the law which commandment was most important. Of course Jesus first cited that we are to love the Lord with all that we have, but he went on in Mark 12:31 to add: *"The second is this: 'Love your neighbor as yourself.' There is no commandment greater than these."* As I spoke those words to him, I instantly saw that I had hit a nerve! He looked at me with such anger. He was fuming. His eyes narrowed and he snarled, "I hate my neighbor as much as myself." His eight words summed up his bitterness with astounding clarity! I quietly reminded him that I had been a drill instructor and had "gotten into people's faces too…you are not intimidating me, brother!" We had a lot of work to do! After hours of talking together and unpacking his pain, he came around and realized that the bitterness was hurting him, not his neighbor! Bitterness is like unforgiveness in that it rots our hearts; it's an emotional type of cancer. It isolates us and causes others to keep away. Who pets an angry dog, after all?

A headline of an article written by Shari Roan, in the *Los Angeles Times*, caught my eye: "Bitterness as a mental illness?" It was sub-headed: "Bitter behaviour is so common and deeply destructive that some psychiatrists are urging it be identified as a mental illness under the name post-traumatic embitterment disorder."[15] I commend the article to you. I found it on the internet.[16] German psychiatrist, Dr. Michael

---

[15] Used with permission: LA Times

[16] http://articles.latimes.com/2009/may/25/health/he-bitterness25.

Linden, is quoted extensively throughout the article and is credited with naming this disorder and advocating for an official diagnosis of post-traumatic embitterment disorder (PTEB). In my ministry, however, I see bitterness as an outgrowth of PTSD and personally believe that the pathway to healing is the same as in healing PTSD. Interestingly, I did an internet search on Google for "bitterness" in March 2011 and found 11,000,000 references! Astounding as that is, when I then did the same for "stress", over 222,000,000 references popped up. This helped confirm for me that stress is the overarching issue of our day, while bitterness is one of many debilitating by-products of stress disorders.

Having said that, I do not mean to diminish the importance of overcoming bitterness. It is of supreme importance to acknowledge its existence as a side effect and to also seek healing for this dis-ease. There is much evidence of how damaging it is. But in addition to the wisdom gleaned through scientific studies, I happen to know the Wisdom that comes from God. I have seen Him heal bitterness. If we try to separate from PTSD, the various direct responses to trauma memories that occur in PTSD sufferers (such as bitterness), it can add another hurdle rather than pave a new pathway to healing. For our purposes in this book, we must deal with the impact and the collateral damage of bitterness as a side effect of PTSD. It should give us great comfort to know that there is nothing new under the sun! Our Creator God has known about bitterness from the beginning of time and He has given us every resource necessary to overcome its damage.

Have you ever suffered a head cold or a sinus infection? It starts out with sneezing and sniffling and a runny nose. We think we have a handle on it. We use our favorite cold remedy that we believe in and faithfully practice our cold remedy protocols. But in time our nose which once leaked thin, clear mucus, is now filled with a thicker, opaque variety. (Sorry, I know this sounds disgusting.) So now we must blow our noses to breathe. We also avoid people and places because we feel toxic. Over time, the volume of mucus increases, it's endless! One wonders where all this stuff is stored? Our poor noses become raw and cracked. Our heads ache and no matter how often we blow our noses, there is always more! Ultimately the mucus goes down our throats, congests our lungs and produces painful coughing. Colds come and go in their own time. Though we try to remedy them, we cannot cure them.

Well, that is pretty much how bitterness appears to the one who holds it and who is held captive by it. An embittered person doesn't set out to be bitter. Its presence followed a situation or event for which they have residual anger or latent resentment. Bitter people do not think that their bitterness is out of their control. They even take certain precautions to contain it—avoiding certain people, places, experiences and so on, in an attempt to reduce its impact. Some follow protocols that make them believe they can remedy it. But eventually it spreads throughout the whole person. Before long it infects every area of their lives. It is fantasy to believe that bitterness and its impact can be controlled by an act of will. Endless supplies of bitterness can be stored in our brains. Bitterness is tucked away with trauma memories, along with the memory of specific responses that have been triggered. But unlike a cold, it never goes away on its own.

Unfortunately, no one is bitterness resistant. In fact, it is quite easy to become embittered. We may hold bitterness against our parents, our siblings, our neighbors, our spouse, our co-workers, our priest, our pastor, our boss, and even against God. We are prone to this dis-ease that is like a cancer eating away at the essence of our souls. The Merriam-Webster On line Dictionary describes bitterness as: *bitter, distasteful or distressing to the mind; marked by intensity or severity; accompanied by severe pain or suffering; being relentless determined; exhibiting intense animosity; harshly reproachful, marked by cynicism and rancor; intensely unpleasant; expressive of severe pain or grief or regret.*

There is nothing contained in bitterness that is life-giving or joy-filled, nothing in this condition that would make it desirable; and yet embittered people cannot let go of it. In Jonah 2:8 in the Old Testament of the Bible, it says: *"Those who cling to worthless idols forfeit the grace that could be theirs."* As we shall see, God understands bitterness and He knows that it must be healed. When embittered people hang onto bitterness and refuse to let go of it, they refuse the grace of God. However, when sufferers become willing to accept God's help, He is able to help them overcome all of the negativity that is associated with bitterness.

Bitterness is referenced only nineteen times in the New International Version 1984, ©1984 of the Bible; not nearly as many times as I would have expected. Surprisingly, there is not one mention of bitterness in any of the four Gospels. The closest inference to it can be found in Luke 9:5: *"If people do not welcome you, shake the dust off your feet when you leave their town, as a testimony against them."* It is comforting to know that even the disciples encountered people who were unkind and unwelcoming to them. If on the surface it might appear that Jesus was endorsing an embittered response to rejection in this passage, we need to look at it again and recognize the wisdom He is imparting to us. "Shaking the dust off" is a physical response that can help us to cope with rejection in a more emotionally healthy way. I think Jesus is saying that when we encounter something that can cause us to be bitter, we need to walk away from it, leaving behind anything that may have attached itself to us; even the dust on our feet! Jesus' advice: Take nothing with you from a negative experience. Shake it off, let it go! Don't even open the door to the possibility of bitterness!

While the Gospels may not speak directly to it, bitterness is mentioned most in the Book of Job. No surprise there. The references in Job, however, all speak to the "bitterness of the soul". Not bitterness of the mind, or even of the heart, but that which is deeply rooted in the soul. Take a look at Job 10:1: *"I loathe my very life; therefore I will give free rein to my complaint and speak out in the bitterness of my soul."* These words of Job sting and we can hear raw pain and despair oozing from his soul. Is this the face of bitterness? What should we do with it? I must ask you to consider your answer to this question: do you want to be bitter or better? Further on in Job (21:25) we read: *"Another man dies in bitterness of soul, never having enjoyed anything good."* That verse pierced my soul. Do I want to die with bitterness in my soul? No thanks!

At the end of the Book of Job, we learn that Job prayed for his "friends" (the very people who had contributed to his bitterness of the soul). In his simple act of praying, in earnest, for his not-so-kind-friends, we see Job "shaking the dust off" and letting go of his bitterness. This simple act delights the heart of God. In the last chapter of this lengthy account of loss, suffering, despair and bitterness, we encounter a faithful God, Who blesses Job abundantly. Check out what our God does in the following verses found in Chapter 42: (v.10) *"After Job had prayed for his friends, the LORD made him prosperous again and gave him twice as much as he had before."* (v.12) *The LORD blessed the latter part of Job's life more than the first.* (v.16-17) *"After this, Job lived a hundred and forty years; he saw his children and their children to the fourth generation. And so he died, old and full of years."* Wow! Job got his life back, twofold what he had lost! This is the work of God when we follow His advice.

The book of Job assures us that there is hope for all of us ... for all the Jobs and Job-ettes of this life!

I have met many embittered people in the work that I am called to do. Many of them have been poisoned by others who passed on their bitterness to them. The collateral damage of bitterness gets distributed broadly by those who suffer with it and who somehow find comfort in "sharing" it with others. In Amos 6:12, it is written: *"Do horses run on the rocky crags? Does one plough there with oxen? But you have turned justice into poison and the fruit of righteousness into bitterness—"* Similar to this verse in Amos, embittered people can corrupt what is good or even innocent. In their attempts to qualify and justify their bitterness, they can sour even the sweetest soul. By its very nature, bitterness is not hidden, it is evident to and experienced by all in proximity. Others can see it, taste it, feel it and, sadly, even be spoilt by it.

In Acts 8:23, St. Paul doesn't mix his words when he says, *"For I see that you are full of bitterness and captive to sin."* We can see bitterness and we can see the power it has over people. We can also taste it. We often speak of being left with a "bitter taste" in our mouths when an organization, a church, a business, a parent, a sibling or a friend, hurts us. And what then becomes of that bitter taste that is allowed to remain in our mouths. Well, once again, the words of St. Paul in Romans 3:14: *"Their mouths are full of cursing and bitterness."* And the words of bitter people have power over us.

The last mention of bitterness in the Bible is found in Ephesians 4:31. Paul commands us to: *"Get rid of all bitterness, rage and anger, brawling and slander, along with every form of malice."* Just look at all that is lumped together in that verse; bitterness is linked with rage, anger, brawling, slander and every form of malice! Bitterness will destroy a soul and will infect everyone else around that soul. And bitterness doesn't just affect the mind; it impacts the entire body. It affects what words come out of the mouth, what things are hidden in the heart; and what digs its way deep into the very core of the soul. If you suspect this has happened to you, please get rid of your bitterness before it spreads to even one more person! God wants to deliver us from this toxicity. Following verse 31 of Ephesians, are Paul's words inspired by the Holy Spirit to advise you how to do that. Please read the following from Ephesians 4:32: *"Be kind and compassionate to one another, forgiving each other, just as in Christ God forgave you."* This is the Lord's antidote to bitterness, my friends. Please read it once more in the "King's English," won't you? In the King James Version of the Bible, Ephesians 4:32 reads: *"And be ye kind one to another, <u>tenderhearted</u>, forgiving one another, even as God for Christ's sake hath forgiven you."* Emphasis was added for you! Tenderhearted! How appropriate is that? Can there be any better single word in our language to express the opposite of bitterness? When we are willing to accept God's help, He can heal us of all bitterness. He can soften a hard heart and make it tender!

Is there any bitterness in you today? Why not let it come to the surface and hand it over to the Lord to heal you? How does God tenderize your heart? By forgiving you and helping you to forgive others. Being able to forgive those who have caused bitterness in your life is vitally important. It is Christ's command that we forgive. It's not an option. Have you ever recited the Lord's Prayer? If so, you will have said words similar to, "forgive us our trespasses as we forgive those who trespass against us." In a more modern version of the Lord's Prayer, you may have said, "forgive us our sins as we forgive those who sin against us." Bottom line: Forgive if you want a heart free of bitterness!

This brings me to a tool that is not very often used in a therapist's office, but I commend it to you as I personally find it to be an incredible way to remove the source of bitterness and unforgiveness in your life. It's quite simple, it's actually a question and it goes like this:

"Will you forgive me for the anger and rage I have had against you because of the pain you have caused me?" This three part question can either be said in prayer or directly to a perpetrator who is aware of the way they have wronged you. Even if your perpetrator is dead, you can still be assured that the Lord will hear your earnest prayer and He will bless you with freedom from your bitterness.

As you read this now, is someone or something coming to your mind that has caused bitterness in your soul? If so, let's deal with it right now in prayer. Allow yourself to go to that place of pain with Jesus at your side. If you invite Him to go with you, He will. Ask Jesus to stand between you and the person who wounded you, the perpetrator. Now think of that perpetrator's name, if you know it. If you don't know the name, then just bring their face to mind. And then pray. Name the person and then repeat, "Will you forgive me for the anger and rage I have had against you because of the pain you caused me?" Allow yourself to go to that place of unforgiveness: the bitter root; the root of injustice, the cause of your pain. If you do this with Jesus daily, over the next twenty-one days, repeating this scenario as best you can and praying for healing, you will retrain your mind. No wonder the Bible tells us to "seek first His kingdom" in Matthew 6:33! Placing Jesus immediately between you and the perpetrator of your wound can bring about the healing of bitterness. This is sometimes called inner healing or the healing of memories. It is a very good place to begin the healing process.

Can the Lord heal you of bitterness, resentment,

unforgiveness, anger, animosity, dislike, hatred, annoyance, irritation, fury, rage, antagonism, loathing, ill will, aversion, detesting, revulsion, and disgust? Yes of course He can! Perhaps the first step is to think how you would live and how you would feel if that issue were removed from your very being by the Lord Jesus Christ. If we allow Jesus to become Lord in every sphere of our lives bitterness can be conquered. What would it feel like to let go of those who have caused bitterness within you? Someone once said that "to have a grudge is a reason for living". Oh my, that is truly sad. Bitterness needs to be confessed, exorcised and removed from the mind, the heart, the soul and the body. Did you know that bitterness can cause disease? Oh yes! Un-repented sin, in itself, is a dis-ease.

The day after I presented a talk on bitterness, a divorced mother who had heard me telephoned to talk about her estranged daughter. At the center of her problem was her bitterness against her former husband, the father of her daughter. The mother was so bitter that her daughter refused to come near her. Hatred and seething rage would spew forth against her husband whenever she was in her daughter's presence. The mother recognized how toxic she had become and I certainly could hear the poison in her voice as she spoke. The sad thing was that her pain was justified. Her former husband was not a nice person at all. She told me that hearing my talk the day before, was like having a full length mirror placed in front of her, causing her to "see all my wrinkles!" She knew that when the bitterness was removed, that she would be able to have a relationship with her daughter again. This woman experienced healing through revelation.

My friends, I truly pray that you will do some work on yourself with the Lord. If I have touched a nerve or pushed any buttons in you today, please get on your knees right now and ask the Lord to help you. Perhaps you might even pray this prayer:

Jesus, I need Your help. I am carrying such pain, such unforgiveness such bitterness against _____.
Help me Lord to forgive as You have commanded us to forgive. Help me to let go of the pain. Help me to forgive the perpetrator, the issue, the formation, the memory of what happened that has planted a seed of embitterment within me. Please help me realize the poison that is within me, that I want You to remove from me. Please help me realize that this unforgiveness is causing me more pain and that with Your help, as You have forgiven, I am set free from this painful memory. Amen.

Dear brother or sister, Jesus died that we might have life abundantly. Please let the Lord take your burden so that you may live your life in His abundance! He came to set the captive free. Why wait? Be set free now.

In closing, I want to leave you with a few quotes from a variety of people addressing this topic:

"Bitterness is like cancer. It eats upon the host."
Maya Angelou (Poet, Author)

"Never succumb to the temptation of bitterness."
The Rev. Martin Luther King, Jr.
(Civil Rights Leader)

"It is a simple but sometimes forgotten truth that the greatest enemy to present joy and high hopes is the cultivation of retrospective bitterness."

Sir Robert Gordon Menzies
(Prime Minister of Australia
1939-1942 & 1949-1966)

"There's a lot of bitterness, there's a lot of anger out there. We all have to work hard to heal those wounds."

Rep. Allen Boyd
(former U. S. Congressman).[17]

"Love does not delight in evil but rejoices with the truth. It always protects, always trusts, always hopes, always perseveres. Love never fails."

St. Paul's letter to the Corinthians
(1 Corinthians 12:6-8a,
The Holy Bible)

"Let love cast out all bitterness within you."

Nigel Mumford
(author of this book!)

---

[17] All quotes above were taken from: http://www.brainyquote. com/quotes/keywords/bitterness.html

CHAPTER SIXTEEN

Therapy

"The Rescue: All praise to the God and Father of our Master, Jesus the Messiah! Father of all mercy! God of all healing counsel! He comes alongside us when we go through hard times, and before you know it, he brings us alongside someone else who is going through hard times so that we can be there for that person just as God was there for us. We have plenty of hard times that come from following the Messiah, but no more so than the good times of his healing comfort—we get a full measure of that, too."

2 Corinthians 1:3-4 (The Message)

"The God of All Comfort: Praise be to the God and Father of our Lord Jesus Christ, the Father of compassion and the God of all comfort, who comforts us in all our troubles, so that we can comfort those in any trouble with the comfort we ourselves have received from God."

2 Corinthians 1:3-4

Blessed be the God and Father of our Lord Jesus Christ, the Father of sympathy (pity and mercy) and the God [Who is the Source] of every comfort (consolation and encouragement), Who comforts (consoles and encourages) us in every trouble (calamity and affliction), so that we may also be able to comfort (console and encourage) those who are in any kind of trouble or distress, with the comfort (consolation and encourage-ment) with which we ourselves are comforted (consoled and encouraged) by God.

2 Corinthians 1:3-4
(Amplified Bible)

146

"Blessed be God, even the Father of our Lord Jesus Christ, the Father of mercies, and the God of all comfort; Who comforteth us in all our tribulation, that we may be able to comfort them which are in any trouble, by the comfort wherewith we ourselves are comforted of God."

2 Corinthians 1:3-4
(King James Version)

This passage from 2 Corinthians 1:3-4 is just so good that I had to quote several different Bible translations of the same verses! Each version expresses another aspect of His healing. So many people I talk with have fear, aversion or shame about receiving therapy. I offer these Bible verses to you as an encouragement for your healing. Please read them again and again and let them sink in. Right there before you, contained in those Scriptures, is hard evidence of the justification, clarity and relief that God will bring to others to help you in your journey toward the healing of trauma. There really are people who can help you! God, Himself, will help you! *"...Ask and you will receive..."* (John 16:24). I know that many combat veterans will not seek help from someone who has never been in combat. Veterans tend to doubt that those who haven't been exposed to combat, could understand what they've been through. Even though a therapist might not have experience in combat, they likely have gone through other traumas which qualify them to give abundant help. The causes of trauma are endless, yet the process of healing from trauma is not necessarily dependent upon the cause. We all need someone to come alongside of us and help us through different seasons in our lives. So, if you view therapy as a stigma, think again! Therapy may be just what you need.

Choosing the right therapist is important, of course.

Should a therapist be male or female? Should he or she be Christian? Should the therapist be recommended by a friend or by a physician? Personally I would recommend that your therapist be Christian so that they can offer you God's wisdom in addition to their professional experience. You can find one on line or in the yellow pages. They may advertise that they are Christian in addition to their other credentials. Whomever you choose, however, it is important that you approach therapy as a partnership. It is not like taking your car into an auto mechanic and saying, "Okay, here I am. I need an oil change and a new battery. Fix me." It is great that you have decided that you need help, but your therapist is not going to hoist you onto a lift and "sort you out." Since you must take part, choose wisely. Interview the therapist in advance to decide whether you are a good match. Here are some questions you might ask: "How long have you been a therapist? How does therapy work? Why did you become a therapist? Do you specialize in an area? What is your opinion of war? Can I trust you to help me? Can I trust you with my wounded soul?" Ask questions even if you think the therapist might answer your question with a question! Be proactive, ask whatever you must in order to be comfortable with your choice. Please do not just sit there and expect the "mechanic" to change your sludgy oil!

Over the years I have noticed that a wall often appears in the midst of therapy. It was initially unseen or even unknown, but it was always there. Eventually we bump into this wall and we recognize it as a roadblock between us and the therapist. It threatens us like an IED (improvised explosive device). We stop, try to change the subject and get around that wall. We want to avoid it. We may even get agitated with the therapist and decide that therapy is just not working for us. Our response can be: *this far, no further.* It is at this time that we may bolt. I had a case once where a teenager actually climbed out of the bathroom window to run away! After a while, the teen calmed down and out of a good conscience climbed back in to unlock the bathroom door! Though we may be okay discussing some issues, it is likely that during therapy that we will encounter issues that are "off limits." We may decide that we just can't "go there" and we make it very clear to our therapist that they have crossed our line.

Now in any relationship there comes a time when crossing certain boundaries or encountering certain issues, will become difficult. When that happens, we could simply get up and walk out. But, this moment is a critical part of the healing process and is a pivotal point; make it or break it! Yes, we can leave. We can tell ourselves that we are simply shaking the dust off of our sandals. But I put it to you, it is better to enter through the narrow gate. What do I mean by that? Well, it is like that overworked expression, "the honeymoon is over." At the first sign of tension, we want to run. We tell ourselves, "Whoa, this is just too close to the wound." Though many of us are uncomfortable with confrontation, there are times in life when we need to confront the issue that is causing us pain. We need to lance the boil. Now, if you know this is likely to happen, then you need to make a decision in advance of its occurrence. When my flight/flight button is pushed, will I choose to enter through the narrow gate? We read in Matthew 7:13, *"Enter through the narrow gate. For wide is the gate and broad is the road that leads to destruction, and many enter through it."* In any relationship roadblocks will appear and there will come a time to make a decision. Do I enter through the narrow gate or do I run away from my problems?

If you can, enter through the narrow gate with your therapist, counselor, priest, spouse or friend. Your life can be changed. The fruit is actually on the other side of that wall. But you have to go out on a limb to get the fruit. Once you get on the other side of the wall, you can talk about anything at all. There is freedom once you have overcome that wall or roadblock. I have in my mind an image of an igloo that envelopes you and your therapist as you talk through your issues. Though you have privacy, the issues keep hitting the walls of that igloo and come bouncing back. Every bounce becomes increasingly painful. But when you decide to open the door of the igloo and come out into the open space, the sky is the limit! You are set free to be as transparent as necessary in the healing process. So make a decision beforehand. If you find yourself being bombarded by painful issues inside that igloo, choose to enter through the narrow gate. Walk out of that igloo, through the narrow gate, into an area where there are no boundaries, no limits to what can be discussed in your therapy. You will experience a new transparency and confidence; a wide, open space in your life.

Jesus came to set the captives free. Perhaps it is your time to be set free. Perhaps it is your time to come out of that igloo or whatever else may be blocking you in this life. When you are free, you can be totally honest with yourself and your feelings. I recognize that many who come to me struggle with trust. They test me and try to push me away. They attempt to alienate me. When a supplicant does this, it simply tells me that they have had problems with rejection. In their life there may be a big, brick wall cemented in place which screams to them, "NO ONE is ever going to reject me again!" That wall was firmly placed there to protect against any further abuse, rejection or threat. But one of the chief reasons God sent His only Son, Jesus, was to set the captives free who were hiding behind those walls. Can you even imagine what life will feel like without that burden, without that stress, without the trigger, without the unhealed trauma? Imagine life without the threat of an IED or sniper positions, real or imaginary? What would life be like when you are freed from perpetrators or trauma memories? With God's help you can be freed of from all clear and present dangers that still have power over you.

Please realize this important truth: You are not alone! There are people who may not have been in combat themselves, but who may have been raped, robbed, ritually abused, abandoned, falsely accused, imprisoned, betrayed, cheated on, demeaned, rejected, or who have been _____ (fill in the blank); but they are trained to help you. There are people uniquely gifted and anointed to help you complete the unfinished business of trauma in your mind. You are not alone! There is someone who can come alongside you and bring you to your very own personal armistice day. There is someone who can help you to celebrate a place of freedom. A place of freedom from whatever your war represents to you. A new found place where whatever baggage or buckets of swill you may be carrying can be emptied, put down and left behind. Free indeed!

Take a moment and see yourself in your mind's eye. Are you standing? Are you carrying baggage? What's in those bags? Are you carrying buckets? What's inside those buckets? What have you been carrying around all these years? Whom do you need to forgive? What incidents in your life have too much value? What or who has had too little value due to the extra weight you carry? Now imagine what your life would be like if you could move without carrying those bags or buckets. Picture what it would be like to have your memories healed, released and set free; to have the haunting removed and to be free to live your life liberated from the past.

Another block to seeking therapy can be issues related to trust. If your trust has been broken by someone how can you trust again? In my work, I see this issue nearly every day. If you have difficulty trusting others, however will you trust a therapist? Consider being able to "try less and trust more." This can be a huge gift to your soul. It is likely that trust can grow again with your therapist, counselor or pastor if you are willing to let go. You might even ask that person, "How can I trust you when I have been so wounded?" Just allowing your chosen therapist to answer that question can help break down your walls of self-protection and allow trust to be built between you. In John 14:1, Jesus said: *"Do not let your hearts be troubled. Trust in God; trust also in Me."* If we can trust in Him, then we may also be able to trust those He sends to us. If we trust Him, we can know for ourselves what George MacDonald, Scottish author, poet and Christian minister is quoted to have once said, *"Few delights can equal the presence of one whom we trust utterly."*[18] I pray that you may delight in the presence of a therapist you trust utterly!

You might also protest seeking therapy because you believe that you cannot afford it. Well, though it may be difficult to pay for your therapy, it is important to see it as an investment in your future. Some therapists have a sliding scale fee schedule. Some do not charge at all. Your medical plan may also cover most of the costs of therapy. But please take on a new perspective that every penny you spend is for your soul. You could shop till you drop at the mall, but there is nothing that you can buy there that will heal your soul. Nothing! When you invest in your healing, you are giving yourself a gift: the gift of life, the gift of freedom. You are buying something tangible, though unseen. The effects of

---

[18] http://www.brainyquote.com/quotes/topics/topic_trust. html#ixzz1HMVI9prK

therapy, however, will be evident to everyone!

Often hurting people fall into a trap; the trap of unforgiveness, of not letting go. It is a trap that captures our thoughts and enslaves us to a memory. Memory of pain has power over us and we are firmly trapped. Interestingly, the best way to catch a monkey is to cut a hole in the end of a coconut shell. Tie the coconut with rope to a tree and fill it with peanuts. When a monkey smells the nuts, he squeezes his open hand into the shell to get at those peanuts. His fist now filled with nuts can't back out of that hole in the coconut shell. He's trapped because he won't let go of those peanuts. When trappers come to take him captive, even then—he won't let go of those nuts! Just like that monkey, we insist on holding onto our pain at all costs. We won't let go, even when we realize that we've become imprisoned by it. What do *you* need to let go of in order to be free?

My mentor, the Rev. Canon Jim Glennon, once told me how he dealt with past offenses. He would sit in his prayer chair and pray. He would put anything that bothered him behind him, much as Jesus modeled in Mark 8:33. After doing this for years, he suddenly had an epiphany. Canon Jim stood up and literally turned his chair around to face all the problems he had put behind him. He saw them in a new light. He saw them as Christ did. He realized that there was no power left in anything that was behind him. Those things that had held him captive had been rendered pathetic, shriveled and powerless. He told me that he experienced a great release in that moment.

Pray. Ask God, what it is that you are hanging onto? Ask Him to help you turn and face the issues of the past. Then take those things to a therapist, counselor, pastor or prayer team and share with them what you've been made aware of. Ask God to heal you and to assist those He has brought to you to be His healing hands. Also, read again the

Bible verses at the beginning of this chapter. My heart goes out to you dear soul.

"For everyone who asks receives; he who seeks finds; and to him who knocks, the door will be opened." (Luke 11:10).

Go on now, enter through the narrow gate...

CHAPTER SEVENTEEN

Living with Someone with PTSD

*"For we do not preach ourselves, but Jesus Christ as
Lord, and ourselves as your servants for Jesus' sake."*
2 Corinthians 4:5

*"…If anyone serves, he should do it with the strength
God provides, so that in all things God may be praised
through Jesus Christ…"*
1 Peter 4:11

*"The definition of insanity is doing the same thing
over and over again and expecting different results."*
Albert Einstein

Asleep, I Listen:
A Meditation for Care Givers

"Asleep I listen,
To the breathing, to every precious breath,
To any change, to a groan, to the pain, to the fear,
I listen to the fear, in me, and in my beloved.
Asleep I listen,
To any need and want, my body asleep but my ears
open,
The constant vigil, ready at a moment's notice
To leap out of bed to address the need.
Asleep I listen,
To the phone, to the TV, to the radio, to God.

I pray and wonder what will happen?
Am I doing my best, what else can I do?

Asleep I listen,
Even when awake guilt pervades my mind.
How can I even go to the store, how can I leave the
house?
I listen to the cell phone, did it beep, is it vibrating?
Asleep I listen,
To my faults, to my responsibility, to my blame.
What if? If only! But why God, WHY?
I can't even pray anymore I am so tired.
Asleep I listen,
My mind wonders what will it be like afterwards?
What will I do? Where will I go? How will I live?
Oh NO it's not about me, guilt pervades again.
Asleep I listen,
A friend calls and asks me out for a coffee.
'I will call you back, if there is a change.'
I wonder, can I really step out of the house?
Asleep I listen,
To God,
Who says 'Well done good and faithful servant.'
'Do not be afraid, I am with you always.'
Asleep I listen to my conscience and all is well with my
soul."

The Rev. Nigel W D Mumford

L iving with someone who has been traumatized in life and is suffering from PTSD is good reason to set healthy boundaries. Without healthy communication between spouses, especially if both have suffered trauma, their marriage is at risk of becoming a constant source of triggers.

The axiom, "Of course your family pushes your buttons" comes to mind. Our loved ones know us. They know our quirks, foibles, warts, and everything else! They may not see, with their eyes, the wall that the trauma victim has built but they know its perimeters and, they know when they get too close to the "hot spot." There is a lot of give and take necessary in our relationships, but the spouse of the sufferer of PTSD is mostly the "giver." Living with someone with PTSD is like negotiating our path around an unexploded bomb or walking on egg shells. Their hyper-vigilance can be the source of great tension within family dynamics. The family knows all too well, that the slightest thing can set the victim off. Just like a bomb.

In addition to combat related trauma, which we have explored at length, are those who have been traumatized by sexual abuse. Those suffering from this source of trauma are likely to "freeze up" and have flashbacks. Years ago I met a man who at eight years old was caught by his mother playing with his own genitals. His mother had been very angry and had warned him that he would go blind if he did that. Three weeks later he was blinded in one eye when a friend accidentally hit him in the eye with a pebble lobbed by a sling shot. He determined in his mind that his Mum had been right! When this man and his new wife came to see me a few weeks after they married, they were having major problems. The guilt, the memories of his Mum's angry reaction to him, her shouting at him, and all the issues of unfinished trauma had caused, not surprisingly, impedance in their marriage. I prayed with him for the healing of memories and after several prayer sessions, as well as the collaborative help of a couples' therapist, a place of healing was reached.

When the sufferer of PTSD can talk about life and share their stress and potential triggers, it can strengthen the couple's marriage and the family unit. Whenever possible, it's important for the sufferer to honestly tell their spouse how their spouse can help whenever they're triggered. Would they prefer to be left alone? Would they rather be hugged and held? What would work best for them? How can their spouse help in their fight/flight response, if at all? How can a spouse help without escalating the problem and becoming a victim themselves? Rather than lashing out at loved ones, is it possible for the sufferer to ask for help? Indeed, it may be embarrassing, even difficult, to ask for help. It might also be humbling. But if you, as the PTSD sufferer, can ask for help and even offer guidance as to how others might respond when you're triggered, it can be an important first step in the right direction.

What do I mean by that? In the past when I was triggered and pushed beyond my limit, I would be like a bomb that exploded internally. People could obviously see the change in me at those moments, but recognized that it was an internal war. I think that I am very fortunate that it never resulted in violence. Unfortunately, reacting; whether internally, externally or both, is a way of life for those suffering from PTSD. In the healing process, however, external responses of angry, violent outbursts are walls or roadblocks. If this is the case for you or your spouse, serious boundaries and rules need to be established for the health and safety of each other and others in your immediate family. The bottom line for you, if you are the PTSD victim, is that your spouse is not the enemy. Your spouse is on your side. With the help of God, as well as a good and understanding therapist, the communication between spouses can be improved and peace and healing can be achieved.

Sir Isaac Newton was contemplating the world when an apple fell from a tree and hit him on the head. It was at that moment he realized the effect of gravity. The effect of trauma can cause us to fall just as gravity can. Some of Newton's quotes have helped me in the process of healing: [19]

"*We build too many walls and not enough bridges.*" PTSD sufferers are notorious for building walls! We need to build more bridges!

"*To every action there is always opposed an equal reaction.*" So it is with the process of healing. If pressed too hard, the equal reaction within a spouse can be enormous pain.

"*Tact is the art of making a point without making an enemy.*" PTSD sufferers lose all tact when triggered. Good communication can mitigate the damage of victims' reactions when triggered.

"*A man may imagine things that are false, but he can only understand things that are true, for if the things be false, the apprehension of them is not understanding.*" Such is the void of PTSD and all that it represents: confusion, dis-ease, dissatisfaction, unhealed wounds, and unfinished business.

Non-verbal communication can become a gift to your marriage. As the victim of PTSD you can create a gesture, a discreet signal, to allow greater understanding between you and your spouse. A hand on a head or a right hand touching the right ear lobe, or the index finger on the nose; can become intimate ways to communicate between the two of you. Doing this can send two messages: one message is to the spouse that you are being triggered; and the other is to yourself that you know you're going to "that place." It can also be your spouse who uses a gesture to ask whether you are headed "there?" Giving your spouse permission to "ask" in that discreet manner, allows the PTSD sufferer to be alert to the heightened anxiety in their spouse at any

---

[19] http://www.brainyquote.com/quotes/authors/i/isaac_newton.html

given moment. Reassurance can be immediate when the sufferer simply shakes their head "no." Such communication can do wonders to defuse concern. If the sufferer has been triggered, it can help both spouses put an agreed upon plan into action.

When a sufferer of PTSD can be somewhat transparent and ask for help, mountains of stress can be removed. Asking for help or discussing these things with one's spouse can be a problem for some men who view such activity as a weakness to their manliness. This is, of course, yet another matter for healing and a first step in setting the captive free. Getting over this hurdle will require healing in addition to the trauma itself. As the victim, it is important to remember that your spouse is on your side and you can begin to consider new ways to communicate with them. If you continue to avoid these areas, the "elephant in the room" will possibly sit on both of you!

When triggered, a primary response for the sufferer may be to remove oneself from the situation. Again fight/flight: either a fight will ensue or flight is in the making. Though flight, or leaving, can be very frustrating for the spouse, it may be necessary for safety reasons to allow time for a reaction to defuse. It may require an hour or so, or in the case of some others I know they get in the car and just drive until they can be at peace. This calming down period is the slowing down of the fly wheel.

This type of living can be utterly exhausting and taxing on a marriage, because your enemy still has the upper hand. No, your spouse isn't the enemy! The enemy is the continued horror of memory that the sufferer is trying to sort out in their mind. In trying to get away from that enemy, the PTSD sufferer grieves and pains the spouse or the children who are left behind. We do seem to hurt the ones we love. If the sufferer can admit that their spouse is not their enemy, sharing with their spouse what is going on and developing an understanding between them can eliminate much of the confusion, pain and misplaced guilt when things erupt.

Embracing the gift of communication within a marriage is hard enough without the uninvited guest of PTSD. Extreme grace is required by the spouse to be able to forgive again and again. Changing behaviors can be a slow process but there is hope. After all, with God all things are possible and when the fly wheel is triggered, if nonverbal communication is welcome in a marriage, we could see the depths and breadth of Christ's healing love. If a couple will get on their knees and ask God for help and pray that the enemy will be exposed, healing will take place.

Can this healing be done alone? No, help is needed from a therapist, counselor, pastor or peer group. Reach out and ask for help. You are not alone. Jesus told us and promised, "...Ask and it will be given to you..." (Luke 11:9). If you are being abused, either verbally or physically, it is vitally important to get help. Please remove yourself from the situation. Verbal abuse can escalate to physical abuse, so please remember not to transfer your anger at the perpetrator or the enemy to your spouse or other loved ones. Your spouse is not the enemy! Don't give your enemy or perpetrator that kind of power over you. Simply identifying this can be a huge breakthrough in the process of healing relationships.

It is not easy to live with someone with PTSD, it can be downright difficult. But with grace, love, and honesty, the slow process of healing can begin. Of course, with God's help, healing is evidenced in every aspect of your person and your marriage. I know this personally and of this I am sure by faith. I urge you to set healthy and honest boundaries for yourselves. If face to face communication is a stressor, consider writing letters or emails. Each of those written forms gives you opportunity to review your words carefully so as not to cause more misunderstanding. Consider Proverbs 12:18: *"Reckless words pierce like a sword, but the tongue of the wise brings healing."* Ask your spouse to help you. Remember why you married in the first place! Give the enemy the boot in your household and invite the Lord into your home. Enjoy your life—discover the abundance that Jesus came to give you. There is help. There is a way in, and through, Christ Jesus. With Christ's help everything is possible.

How do we live with someone with PTSD? With great patience, with love, with forgiveness, with communication, with help from a therapist, with help from Christ, with help from God.

If you need help, ask. And if you ask God, have hope. Hear these encouraging words of St. Paul taken from his letter to the Romans 5:5: *"And hope does not disappoint us, because God has poured out His love into our hearts by the Holy Spirit, Whom He has given us."*

CHAPTER EIGHTEEN

Healing Memories/Inner Healing

*"We demolish arguments and every pretension
that sets itself up against the knowledge of God,
and we take captive every thought to make it
obedient to Christ."*
2 Corinthians 10:5

*"How much power, in the present moment,
do we give personally to an incident or person who
has hurt us in the past? Can we allow Christ to take
captive every thought that has wounded us?"*
Nigel Mumford

*"O Christ of the road of the wounded
O Christ of the tears of the broken
In me and with me the needs of the world
Grant me my prayers of loving and hoping
Grant me my prayers of yearning and healing."*
Celtic Prayers from Iona
(A prayer to lead people into
deeper intercession.)

I have since lost the writer's name of the quote below which was taken from Psalm 6 for Holy Week meditations a while ago. It has long been in my heart as a restatement of how I feel about healing ministry and the need for inner healing in the area of abandonment:

"It is Holy to be so passionate about what you believe that you will pass through fear and end your life standing for it. It is Holy to try your best to teach others the truth, to pick them up when they fall away from the truth, and to love them even when they fail in the end. It is Holy not to sell out. It is Holy not to rise to the bait when you are under mortal pressure. It is Holy to be honest about your deepest fears, and even to shake your fist at God when you feel abandoned. All those things Jesus did in the first holy week, long ago. When we walk that week today, can we call it less than holy?"

(Anonymous)

I'm going to focus on the healing of memories, or inner healing, in this chapter. Before we get into the meat of this fascinating subject I want to give you a quiz. Let's say you are driving in your car, it is full of someone's belongings. You cannot remove anything from the car. It is raining very heavily. You come across a bus stop. You only have one seat available in your car. There are three people at the bus stop: 1) a woman in urgent need of medical attention; 2) a friend who previously saved your life; 3) the man or woman who is the love of your life. What would you do?

This chapter is all about thinking differently; thinking "outside of the box." When it comes to inner healing, we have to think outside of the box. Actually when it comes to any aspect of healing ministry, we must think outside the box! I am reminded of a bookstore in Manchester Vermont. On the stone path outside the entrance, it is written "nothing is written in stone." I would only amend that to include: "apart from the ten commandments and a gravestone!"

Now about that quiz. Most of us would likely choose to

take the sick person to the hospital. But if you think outside the box, there may be a better solution. You could put the sick person in the passenger seat and give your car keys to the person who saved your life. You know you can trust that person to drive the sick person to the hospital. Then you can hang out at the bus stop with the person you love until help arrives. Of course this is an unlikely scenario today since someone at that bus stop would have a cell phone with which to call for medical assistance. But hopefully thinking through this quiz can get you to start thinking more globally. As we explore inner healing, it will be important for you to think outside the box.

Inner healing is a process. On one occasion a single prayer session might take care of one situation, while another situation might require several sessions. It is necessary to find a prayer team that is trained and experienced in this type of ministry. If you are the one praying for inner healing of someone, then it is crucial for you to know that it is illegal to suggest to anyone that something happened to them in their past. For instance, those praying for someone must never suggest that the person was abused as a child. Such a suggestion is called "implanting a false memory" and is known as "false memory syndrome." It is against the law! Under no circumstance is it ever appropriate for you or any member of a prayer team to suggest or plant a thought with the one you are praying for, as it may cause them further damage. The history of a supplicant is not your history. Additionally those praying for someone are not investigators assigned to determine the validity of what a supplicant tells them. Memory can be real or perceived, but each person's experience of their memory is real to them and should not be assessed or judged by those who pray for them.

Bad memories are often trapped in the brain. It is as though the information is stored on a DVD disc and can play at will. Buttons are pushed and the trigger is released. The fly wheel is now spinning. Memories that plague, haunt, fester, infect, preoccupy, trouble, disturb, irritate, aggravate, taint, contaminate, possess, obsess, fixate, become a nuisance, cause a danger, upset, worry, bother, concern, agitate, perturb, scare, soil, pollute, sadden and disappoint, infect the brain and everyday life. When buttons of our DVDs get pushed, we can go out of control. We can be transported back to the very "scene of the crime", to a past moment that is instantly made immediate and present. These painful memories mold, guide, shape and serve as a baseline in which we live.

It is entirely possible that what we may have relied upon as a reference point in our lives, is a lie! As kids, my siblings and I would make ugly faces. Our mother would say, "If the wind changes, your face will stay like that for the rest of your life." Of course we immediately stopped making those faces as we didn't want to spend the rest of our lives with our noses pushed up and our tongues sticking out. But think on this a moment. At what age did we realize that our mother's statement was not the truth? Have we used that same lie on our own children? At what age did we realize that this was simply a tactic our mother employed to control our behavior? There are moments when the "light" comes on for us and we recognize that what we had believed to be true, is not true at all! It is then that we begin to realize that the truth sets us free. *"Then you will know the truth, and the truth will set you free."* John 8:32

The good news is that as adults... I'll say that again... as adults (bold, underlined, neon light, pay attention here...) we can, with Christ's help, be given a new baseline or point of reference. That new baseline is TRUTH. Perhaps as we seek to know what part of our memory has really caused us pain and what part of that memory needs to be healed...

we can ask ourselves if we can trust our memory as the truth? Jesus came to set the captives free: *"The Spirit of the Sovereign LORD is on me, because the LORD has anointed me to proclaim good news to the poor. He has sent me to bind up the brokenhearted, to proclaim freedom for the captives and release from darkness for the prisoners."* (Isaiah 61:1) *And we take captive every thought to make it obedient to Christ.* (2 Corinthians 10:5) As we seek truth, we are set free from the past that chains us.

Judith MacNutt tells a wonderful story about a man who goes to a fairground and sees that an elephant's right rear foot is chained to a stake in the ground. The man looks at the chain and then looks at the size of the elephant. He then approaches the handler and says, "I notice that the chain holding your elephant is not very large. It looks to me as though that elephant could break it with just one pull." The handler responded, "Yes, that's true. That's actually the same chain which held him when he was small. It was strong enough then, but it wouldn't hold him now. But he won't even try to break that chain because he remembers that when he was young, he couldn't break it. In his mind he still cannot break it." So it is with the healing of memories. We can be chained to a memory in the same way as the elephant. With the Lord's help, however, we can come to believe that we truly can be set free. We can break free from those chains.

What is inner healing?

Recall that in 2 Corinthians 10:5, *"We demolish arguments and every pretension that sets itself up against the knowledge of God, and we take captive every thought to make it obedient to Christ."* Inner healing is a process through which painful or traumatic memories are taken *"captive"* and made *"obedient to Christ."* Under the guidance of the Holy Spirit Who leads believers into all truth, we are able to uncover wounds and lies that have held us captive through shame, guilt or fear. By going back to a painful memory, accompanied by the Risen Lord Jesus and letting Him speak the Gospel into our hearts, will usher in truth, healing, peace and forgiveness. All people, including those who call themselves Christian, are adversely affected by what is said and what is done to them. Over the years if hurtful words and actions are not surrendered to Christ and if His Light is not allowed to shine on them, they will fester like emotional cancers. Eventually they will surface and reveal themselves as anxiety, depression, addictions, compulsivity, inability for intimacy, chronic anger, eating disorders, sexual confusion and so on.

Inner healing often addresses the root cause of those emotional cancers that have festered. As the Holy Spirit leads, He is able to pinpoint the core source of emotional affliction and He will speak the truth to the part of the soul that is wounded, captive or bound. As healing continues over time, people begin to realize that they are being freed from what had once held them captive. Once again we hear the words of Luke 4 18-19, *"He has sent me to proclaim freedom for the prisoners and recovery of sight for the blind to release the oppressed and to proclaim the year of the Lord's favor."* Imagination is God's gift to us through the power of the Holy Spirit. In using our imagination, we can see Jesus present in our memory and experience painful events submitting to His authority as Lord. While inner healing cannot change the hurtful things as they actually happened to us, it does allow God to heal the damaged emotional and spiritual effects of the past. Inner healing changes the way we look and respond to our wounded past.

My visual picture of inner healing is seeing Jesus

remove the stored DVD in the mind, laying His hands on it and then returning it, not erased, but healed. The DVD has the word "HEALED" printed over each frame as a reminder. Jesus doesn't erase our memory because it is part of who we are. Instead, He heals the memory. The DVD is still operable, but it no longer contains the triggers that produce the sweats, the thousand yard stares and other physical and/ or emotional reactions. Memories, therefore, are reframed by Christ as He is invited into them. Inner healing is really a revelation of 'The Truth.' Hear again the words of John 8:32-33, *"Then you shall know the truth and the truth will set you free. They answered him, "We are Abraham's descendants and have never been slaves of anyone. How can you say that we shall be set free?"* According to the Scriptures, is it possible then, that we can be a slave to a memory?

Perhaps this is a good time for you to pause and reflect on what you have just read. Ask yourself whether you have memories which have kept you captive? This is where your unpacking needs to begin so that you can get to the heart of the artichoke. A good start might be to construct a list of memories that have plagued you. Are there recurrent memories or flashbacks which haunt you? As you seek help for healing, consider whether you can define your relationship with specific memories. Are you linked, chained or bound to them just as the elephant was? Can you even imagine what life would be like without that memory having power over you?

To put this thought in a more contemporary framework we can think of it in computer terms. Is there a hyperlink, on your brain's hard drive, to an issue that is ruling and ruining your life? Do you have a worm or virus that's running interference in your ability to analyze input and output? Do you need a "control-alt-delete" button in order to be rid of it? Or do you need to upload an anti-virus program to sweep your brain clean? If this modern metaphoric language is helpful, then consider that Jesus Christ is the ultimate anti-virus program! He is not only willing to do the job, but He is the only One Who could possibly succeed at permanently healing your mind.

Does the memory that you find yourself tethered to have an audible component where you hear, "Do not tell anyone about this or I will kill you!" Are you so enslaved by a memory, that when it surfaces you find yourself reacting to it as though it is a recent occurrence? Take for example my negative response to the smell of chocolate. You may recall the bomb blast at the chocolate factory that traumatized me when I was on active duty in the military. Well five miles down the road from where we used to live was a chocolate factory. Even knowing exactly what the trigger was and what my response would be, I would still "go there" every time I drove by that factory. I really like to eat chocolate, but something negative nudged me every time I drove by! Though I did not pay much attention to this regular event, I found myself feeling uncomfortable whenever that smell would enter my car.

One day, I was driving my father somewhere when I was totally overcome by that scent. I immediately pulled the car off the road near the main gate. My father asked me what I was doing. Out of the blue, I spoke without even thinking and shared all about one of the worst bomb blasts in my combat experience. It was then that I realized that I was captive to a memory with unfinished business which needed to be dealt with. With my car stopped, I just sat there and told my father the whole story. After that, the smell of that chocolate factory had no power over me. It was as if the memory had been defused, unlike the bomb that had exploded years ago. Another memory put to rest, one that I had hidden for years: the realization that I was very lucky to have survived that blast. That subterranean memory had, had power over me until the light of truth was shone upon it when I told my story to my father. I was set free.

Sometimes a memory, whether true or false, can be so imbedded that we do not even recognize that there is an underlying problem. That is, of course, until Christ is invited into that memory. When Jesus sheds His light upon a memory and ushers in His truth, He "sets the captives free!" It doesn't matter whether we are struggling with something that we know as truth or or something that's based upon a lie. Regardless of its origin, the memory needs to be reset or recast so that we will cease responding to it in the same harmful way. Does the name Pavlov ring a bell? Ivan Pavlov was a Russian physiologist who discovered "conditional reflex" while studying the tendency of dogs to salivate in response to food stimuli. Today, the term "Pavlov's dog" describes a person who reacts to a stimulus without forethought. Is that not exactly what happens when a memory is triggered and we instantaneously react in a certain way? In my case, the smell of chocolate did not make me salivate, but the smell triggered an olfactory memory of that bomb blast. Unlike the elephant, I am no longer chained to that memory!

God has given us the gift of free will, a blessing which grants to us the ability to live the way we choose. This amazing gift, or as some may see it: living without His interference; is a wonderful gift for the most part. Problems arise when individuals or groups choose to do something that hurts others as they strive to achieve their own desires. This is the intersection of good and evil where cruelty, or man's inhumanity to man, emerges as the bully, the terrorist, the murderer, the serial killer or the suicide bomber. Many have asked where was God when those airplanes flew into the World Trade Center? Several books have been written on this very subject. But that act was not God's agenda. God was not guilty. That agenda was established by misguided people who believed that they were "putting the world right."

Was God there on 9/11? Oh yes. Was Christ watching in horror and the deepest grief as He witnessed man's inhumanity to man that day? Oh yes. There are five references in the Bible that attest that God will never leave us or forsake us. The first reference is found in Deuteronomy 31:6, *"Be strong and courageous. Do not be afraid or terrified because of them, for the LORD your God goes with you; he will never leave you nor forsake you."* Here the Bible is telling us not to be afraid or terrified, because the Lord is with you. The other four references are in Deuteronomy 31:8, Joshua 1:5, 1 Kings 8:57 and Hebrews 13:5. We're told five times that God will never leave us or forsake us. So here is the rub: I am frequently asked, by those I minister to, "Well Fr. Nigel, where was God when I was raped?" or "Where was God when my son was murdered?" or "Where was God when those hijacked airplanes changed history?" We must remember that the amazing gift of free will that God has given you and me, affords men the opportunity to act in a manner of their own choosing. God doesn't make us do these things, God gives us the ability to choose what we do and who we do it to. So when we choose violence and abuse against one another, God is grieving right alongside of us.

Of course, as we would expect, when the conversation turns to this aspect of God's gift of free will, it can very quickly escalate to anger at God. We can hear ourselves screaming out to Him, "Where were You God when I needed You the most?" We even find references to inferred perplexity and intense emotion as felt by others many times in the Bible. The words of Psalm 115:2 seem to parallel what was close to our minds on 9/11: *"Why do the nations say, 'Where is their God?'"* Also close to our sentiments are the words of Psalm 42:3: *"My tears have been my food day and night, while people say to me all day long, 'Where is your God?'"* And the words found in Psalm 42:10: *"My bones suffer mortal agony as my foes taunt me, saying to me all day long, 'Where is your God?'"* And which believer in Christ cannot relate to the prayer demands of Psalm 79:10: *"Why should the nations say, 'Where is their God?' Before our eyes, make known among the nations that you avenge the outpoured blood of your servants."* Thus taking the war from downtown New York to Iraq and onto Afghanistan.

Looking back at Psalm 42:10 when the psalmist laments that his bones are in mortal agony as his enemies taunt him "Where is your God?", we need to know, in the words of that famous radio broadcaster Paul Harvey, "the rest of the story." The rest of the story can be found in the next verse! Psalm 42:11 goes on to say, *"Why are you downcast, O my soul? Why so disturbed within me? Put your hope in God, for I will yet praise him, my Saviour and my God."* Or we can find the "rest of the story" in the following passage from the prophet Micah 7:10: *"Then my enemy will see it and will be covered with shame, she who said to me, 'Where is the LORD your God?' My eyes will see her downfall; even now she will be trampled underfoot like mire in the streets."* And finally, read these explanatory words of the prophet Malachi 2:17: *"You have wearied the LORD with your words. 'How have we wearied him?' you ask. By saying, 'All who do evil are good in the eyes of the LORD, and he is pleased with them' or 'Where is the God of justice?'"* These verses tell me that God is not absent and is fully aware of man's inhumanity to man ever since Cain and Abel.

We know that God is always with us because He says so. And if we know that even though He grants us free will, He grieves alongside of us when we are subjected to cruelty; then we can begin to understand how essential His presence is when we are seeking truth in the process of inner healing. The key to inner healing is the revelation of truth through Christ, which is freedom. I believe that this is accomplished when prayer partners in listening, loving and praying, guide the supplicant into the truth and the love and the very real compassion of Jesus. Freedom and healing is accomplished when in His presence we experience what Paul wrote in 2 Corinthians 10:5, *"We demolish arguments and every pretension that sets itself up against the knowledge of God, and we take captive every thought to make it obedient to Christ."*

So just how do we "take captive every thought and make it obedient to Christ?" It is important for us to walk through exactly what happens in the healing of memories. The memory is 'replayed' in a safe environment without the interference of telephones, television, radio, pets, or anything else that would distract or interrupt this time. At least two prayer team members, trained in listening, should be present with one of them chosen to lead. A gentle and understanding voice is essential on the prayer team, one that is void of all judgment, surprise, sappy sympathy or aversion. The prayer team should brief the supplicant that they're on the supplicant's side; that there is no hypnosis or other mind controlling mechanism involved; that they'll stop at any time the supplicant indicates that they are uncomfortable; and that they rely upon the very promise that Christ is with us always, just as He was at the time of the "incident" at issue.

During the session, the supplicant is asked by the lead member of the prayer team to recall a memory that needs healing. Now this is can almost be like a flashcard in the mind of the supplicant. It will be a memory that simply jumps out in their mind. This particular memory may not be the main, or core, memory which has been the source of struggle for the supplicant, but that's just fine. Sometimes a less significant, or minor, memory may be a great way to "test drive" healing. In any event, the prayer team must allow the supplicant and Jesus to lead the direction that the prayer session takes. May I also remind the prayer team that they are to listen, love and pray?

The supplicant is asked to close their eyes and place their feet flat on the floor. There is then a time of silence, prayer and a reminder that Jesus is present just as He tells us He has always been. (*"I am with you always!"* Matthew 28:20) The prayer team enters into prayerful conversation when the supplicant is ready. The supplicant is asked to tell their story which is related to which memory they recalled when asked earlier. A timeline is then established: date, location, weather, important details and anything else that would help the supplicant be present one more time in that memory. The scene is set. The supplicant tells the story until the prayer team gently asks the supplicant to stop the DVD of the mind, usually at the ground zero moment when their pain first surfaced. This is the crucial part of inner healing. The supplicant should be handled very gently with the compassion of Christ. Prayer team members must remember that they have a soul in their hands. To return, with Jesus and the supplicant, to the epicenter of a painful memory for the purpose of healing, is such a privilege.

At the moment the supplicant is asked to stop telling the story of their memory, they are asked to look around for Jesus in their mind's eye. I confess that I always wonder whether the supplicant will see Him. I always have a brief moment of doubt in my mind. If you sense such doubt in your team, I recommend praying like the father in Mark 9:24 *"I do believe, help me overcome my unbelief."* Nothing wrong with that! It is very important to be clear Who is doing the healing in a prayer session and to remind ourselves that we must decrease so that He may increase (John 3:30).

Even after twenty years of inner healing ministry, the moment at which the supplicant becomes aware of Jesus' presence is still utterly amazing to be a part of. The supplicant is gently asked to look around the scene, taking a 360 degree view of their memory. It is rather like a detective looking closely at the details, finding clues that help solve their case. As they report their findings the prayer team may observe sweating, tears, shaking, wringing of hands or other external reactions in the supplicant. I personally recommend that the members of the prayer team keep their eyes open, looking for visual prompts and pointers. Watch the face of the supplicant. When the supplicant sees Jesus present in their memory, you may hear, "Wow. You do care, You are there, You do love me!" So many people suffer from rejection, at moments like these the Lord is able to reassure the supplicant that He truly will never leave or forsake them.

Sometimes the supplicant can see the Lord right away during a prayer session, while at other times it may take longer. It is okay to encourage them to keep looking. The prayer team should not give up but may gently suggest that the supplicant look deeper. In the context of the supplicant's memory, encourage them to look through a window or at a surrounding area, to actively seek His presence. To the best of my knowledge the process I've just described was originally taught by Agnes Sanford and was, later, fine-tuned by Frances and Judith MacNutt as they observed supplicants who remained trapped in horrific memories. Healing ministers listen to the guidance of the Lord in the healing process and find ways to make it possible for captives to be freed.

The prophet Isaiah described and foretold of the coming of the Lord Who will open eyes that are blind, free captives from prison and release from the dungeon those who sit in darkness (Isaiah 42:7). Several chapters later, in Isaiah 49:9, the prophet is quoted, *"to say to the captives, 'Come out,' and to those in darkness, 'Be free!' They will feed beside the roads and find pasture on every barren hill."* And in Isaiah 61:1, the prophet refers again to the Year of the LORD's Favor, *"The Spirit of the Sovereign LORD is on me, because the LORD has anointed me to proclaim good news to the poor. He has sent me to bind up the broken-hearted, to proclaim freedom for the captives and release from darkness for the prisoners."* Jesus Himself repeats the words of Isaiah and shocked those who were there as He proclaimed the very same words, *"The Spirit of the Lord is on me, because he has anointed me to proclaim good news to the poor. He has sent me to proclaim freedom for the prisoners and recovery of sight for the blind, to set the oppressed free."* Luke 4:18

So there we have Christ's promise to proclaim the good news to the poor and freedom for the prisoners, even those imprisoned by traumatic memories. Whether a victim of war, rape, genocide, terrorism, bullying, natural disaster, or … you may fill in the blank with your own unique disappointment and trauma; it's so important to know that we can be set free from those memories. Regardless of how long you have been held captive you can be released and set free. Do I believe that healing of memories is formulaic? Well, yes and no. On the one hand inner healing is entirely personal and individualistic. However if there is any formula involved at all, it is found in Christ's love and the Bible verses I've quoted throughout this book. This type of healing takes patience, gentleness and a deep understanding of human need and condition. A healing prayer session can take a couple of hours or just a few minutes.

At a healing service I led in Northern Ireland in 2008, a bank manager had a total meltdown. I assured him that the Lord was with us and that freed him to tell his story about having been robbed five times. The last time he had been robbed his mind had been seared by the memory of a pistol in his mouth and the frenzied screaming and threats of the bank robber. With over fifty people present at our healing service, this bank manager broke down as he told his story, having been so tormented by this memory. I very quickly told him about inner healing and asked him to go back to that horrifying moment and find Jesus in the midst of that bank robbery. It was astounding to see the total transformation of this man as the peace of the Lord came upon him immediately. He became calm and peaceful and even smiled as he was being set free by the Lord. The power of the perpetrator was totally defused by the presence of the Christ.

In a private prayer session in which I was teamed with a prayer partner, a British engineer told the story of his Mum's passing in a hospital. He was such a broken man; broken because he had been the health proxy for his mother and the hospital had advised that there was nothing more that they could do for her. When the time came to switch off her life support, he signed the form. His mother died with all the family present. In the months that followed, his family grew to hate him, blaming him for her death. Even though the doctors had said that they could do nothing more for her, this man became the subject and target of their anger in the course of their grief. This man was so broken. When we got to the moment of turning off the life support in his story, it took a very long time for this British engineer to see the Lord present in that hospital room. In addition to being so British, this poor chap's engineering background kept him "in his head" and it took him longer to process matters of the heart. He was broken, even tortured by this memory and he found it very difficult to talk about it. I asked him to put his DVD on hold and to "look for Jesus." He saw nothing, I told him to look all around the hospital bed and outside the ICU room. I asked him to please look hard for Jesus. Still nothing. Then I found myself singing, "Open the eyes of my heart Lord…" I asked this man to stop looking with his mind and to begin to look with his heart. When he did just that, it was at that moment that this captive was set free. To my astonishment, he looked forward, as if looking at his mother; but then he physically turned to his right and looked on the floor. I expected him to report that he saw Jesus tending his Mum, but I was very wrong. He shared that Jesus was standing over his sister who was curled up in the fetal position on the floor of the ICU sobbing uncontrollably. He said that his Mum was already in heaven but that Jesus needed to console his sister. His vision reflected the real compassion of Christ. What he saw and shared was spoken from the heart, not from his mind! When he left our prayer session, he was a totally different man from the one who had walked in previously. He had been set free!

It matters not how intelligent you are, or how wealthy, or how you look at yourself, or judge yourself or where you rank yourself on the self-esteem scale. The compassion and presence of Christ is always with us even when we are convinced that He is nowhere to be found. It does not matter the amount of wisdom you possess; what matters is how much of Christ's love you have in your heart. And not even that is your responsibility as it is the Lord Who fills your empty heart with His love! Recall the words of St. Paul in Romans 5:5: *"And hope does not disappoint us, because God has poured out his love into our hearts by the Holy Spirit, whom he has given us."* The grace that Jesus Christ has for you is so wonderful because there's nothing you can do to earn it nor is there anything you can do that would send Jesus packing! His grace is a free gift!

Having said that, however, I must clearly state that healing is a process and the supplicant must be ready. The supplicant must be ripe for healing! Healing cannot be imposed upon anyone, it cannot be pushed on anyone nor should it be rushed. The goal is always to set captives free, just as Saint Paul was freed from jail. When someone wants to be healed, the Lord is creative and unstoppable in how He accomplishes it. The power of the enemy is defused. There are times when He may use the jailers' own keys in order to obtain freedom for those who ask. Prayer team members are ambassadors for Christ, doing His bidding by giving aid to the downtrodden. St. Paul wrote in 2 Corinthians 5:20, *"We are therefore Christ's ambassadors, as though God were making his appeal through us. We implore you on Christ's behalf: Be reconciled to God."* Inner healing and the healing of memories promote reconciliation by providing for forgiveness and the infusion of Christ into those painful memories, allowing Him to rewrite our DVDs.

My former mentor, Canon Jim Glennon of Sydney, Australia, once told me a story that has remained forever etched in my mind, as if I had been there when it took place. Canon Jim was a newly ordained curate when he was invited to minister to a couple who lived in a high rise apartment. The couple's baby had crawled off their fifth floor balcony and plunged to his death. The couple, as you would imagine, was just devastated. As Canon Jim approached their building he came upon a couple of people who were talking about what had happened and he overheard someone say, "It was God's will that the child should die, God called him to be one of His angels." Canon Jim paused and said a brief prayer. Then he quietly shared with these strangers that it was not God's will that the child should die, it was man's stupidity in not childproofing the balcony. Canon Jim was a man of few words, but those he spoke were truthful and were intended to reveal God's nature. Canon Jim then went on to share with them that Jesus was right there...weeping with the parents.

I was listening with a woman who had been raped at 8 years of age and left to bleed to death. In recalling the memory she was obviously very disturbed and troubled. After she had shared her full story, I asked her to look for Jesus. She said she could not see him. I prayed, "Lord please reveal Yourself to this woman." Nothing. My faith started to waver. I asked her to describe the room in detail. It was her bedroom. As she narrated what she was seeing, she came to an area that was black. Nothing. Then she went on to describe the room in detailed completion, except for that very dark area of the room. I was perplexed. I prayed silently in my mind, "Where are You, Jesus? We need You, Lord." I prayed my favorite prayer, "HELP." I observed the woman's face as it began to change from a face of terror and pain to a face of jaw-dropping joy. She told me that the area that had been black was now filled with light. She saw a man in the center of it, illuminating the whole area. She told me it was Jesus. She could now see and remember all that was in that corner: her toys, the bookshelves, the pictures on the wall, everything. She had tears of joy. Indeed, Jesus was there! She realized that Jesus had witnessed that horrible incident. She now knew that he wanted her to be healed and to know that He loved her. With Christ present, the memory of that incident was changed miraculously and so was the woman herself!

In 1999 I prayed with an elderly WWII Sergeant who told me that he reckoned he had killed about three thousand people during combat. He had managed to live fifty-four years without experiencing any problems. Then 9/11 happened. When he opened the newspaper and saw the headline, "Three Thousand Suspected Dead", he broke down and was taken to hospital. The flashbacks were unbearable. He felt condemned by the words "three thousand" in that headline. When we prayed together for his inner healing, the Spirit of the Sovereign Lord came upon that man. Generally speaking, it has been my experience that it can take up to three years following trauma or combat before the symptoms of Post-Traumatic Stress Disorder emerge. This man had kept his trauma bottled up for fifty four years! Healed, he is now at peace!

Another American serviceman came to see me in 2004. He had a pronounced bend in his back and he looked very unhappy, as though he was carrying a huge burden. He told me that he had been at the Pentagon on 9/11 and that he'd just been diagnosed with PTSD. Before asking how I should pray for him, it was obvious from his body language that he was a broken man. He told me that he had been at his desk on September 11, 2001 when the alarm had gone off. He had been on call as part of the rescue team and he had followed protocol. But there had been nothing to rescue. When it seemed to be the right time, I had him stop the DVD of his mind and I asked him to look around for Jesus. "Where are You, God?" he asked. He looked to his left, he looked straight ahead and then he pulled back as if the heat from the crash site was too intense, but he kept on looking. Then his face changed. He said, "I see Him." I asked, "Where is He?" Smiling, the man said, "He is standing on a raised mound overlooking the Pentagon." I asked, "What is He doing?" He replied, "Weeping at man's inhumanity to man." As we prayed later, he was still smiling when we suddenly heard a noise as if his spine had popped. His military posture was restored to him. The weight of his burden had been removed. That's why I keep my eyes open during prayer, to watch God at work. He walked out of that prayer room, upright and very different, his healing journey had begun.

As I conclude this chapter on inner healing, I am reminded of Psalm 23. It is interesting to know that the noses and mouths of sheep are quite close together. Sheep are very cautious when it comes to drinking water, because they don't want to get water up their noses. They will drink from a pool or a slow running stream but they avoid drinking from rough waters. Like us, they just don't like water up their noses! In this psalm, we hear the love of God in His provision for all His creation. Take a look at Psalm 23:1-4 with me now: *"The LORD is my shepherd, I shall not be in want. He makes me lie down in green pastures, he leads me beside quiet waters, he restores my soul. He guides me in paths of righteousness for his name's sake. Even though I walk through the valley of the shadow of death, I will fear no evil, for you are with me; your rod and your staff, they comfort me."* He leads the shepherd beside still waters so that the sheep can safely drink. The Lord, as our Shepherd, provides everything necessary to help us receive from His living waters. He prepares a place of peace for us. Are you willing to allow the Shepherd to lead you to the still waters where He can heal you?

I heard a story about something that took place in Africa many years ago. Some white missionaries hired local villagers to carry their equipment to another village. The hired locals were constantly being pushed to go faster and to hurry up so the missionaries could get to the next village. Eventually the hired hands stopped and refused to go any further. The missionaries asked what the problem was. The villagers who had been hired replied, "It is not wise to go so quickly, we have moved too fast, yesterday and today. We must stop and wait here for our souls to catch up with our bodies."

Perhaps we can view inner healing from the African villagers' perspective. Those in need of healing must be ready to receive it. Those who pray for others to be healed must be patient and allow hearts and souls to catch up with the minds of supplicants. Jesus said, "Ask." Ask Him to make you ready. Ask Him to lead you beside the still waters. Ask the Shepherd to heal you from those painful and menacing memories. Just ask.

CHAPTER NINETEEN

Trauma from Life-Threatening Disease

"This was to fulfill what was spoken through the prophet Isaiah: He took up our infirmities and carried our diseases.'"
Matthew 8:17

"O LORD my God, I called to you for help and you healed me. O LORD, you brought me up from the grave; you spared me from going down into the pit. Sing to the LORD, you saints of his; praise his holy name. His favor lasts a lifetime; weeping may remain for a night, but rejoicing comes in the morning."
Psalm 30:2-5
(Psalm 30 for thanksgiving for healing from grave illness.)

It all started with a cough. I had been in the United Kingdom speaking at a military conference on post-traumatic stress. Upon my return, I met up with my wife in New York City for a couple of days and then caught a plane to Jacksonville, Florida to speak on PTSD at a week-long advance training session for the Christian Healing Ministry's School of Healing Prayer©, Level Four. When I arrived at the hotel and checked into my room it was very stuffy and smelled dank. I inspected the air conditioner and saw that is was very dirty. I knew that I should have changed rooms. I actually felt like I was being "told" to change rooms. But I did not. I am not one to make a fuss; looking back, perhaps I should have!

I have no idea where I contracted what doctors eventually diagnosed as H1N1, the swine flu. I could have been exposed anywhere, how do we ever know where we caught a cold? I can tell you, however, that later on many people told me that I had been working too hard and that had caused the H1N1. And I will tell you that, that was not helpful! Hearing those words became a huge irritant to me. I received it as nasty condemnation, as though I was being told that it was my own fault that I had contracted the swine flu!

The weather wasn't great either. It rained cats and dogs the first day of the training conference. Attendees found themselves getting drenched during the lunch break and then re-entering the hotel's frosty air conditioning necessary in Florida. Whilst there, I began coughing. I just didn't feel like myself. By the end of the conference on Friday I was coughing a lot on the flight home. I got home at midnight and my nasty cough just would not stop. Somehow I managed to sleep until 5:00 o'clock in the morning. I was coughing so much that my wife suggested that we take a trip to Saratoga Hospital. Since it was the weekend, she reasoned I would need to be treated at the hospital and it would be quieter in the middle of the night than later on the next morning.

We were given a room and I was seen. The doctor thought I had adult onset asthma, gave me a breathing treatment and sent me home with a puffer. We grabbed some breakfast and then went home. But soon after returning home, the coughing became uncontrollable. I just could not stop. I took a puff of the medication that was given to me by the hospital and instantly fell to the ground gasping for breath. I have to say it was absolutely terrifying. I imagine my eyes and facial expression must have telegraphed fear, even though I felt a certain inner calm. I do recall believing that I was going to die but even so, the peace of the Lord was definitely there. I just couldn't catch my breath, every time I inhaled it created another chronic spasm in my lungs. My wife called for an ambulance right away. I was now in the fetal position trying desperately to breathe and unable to speak. I was gasping for life.

Soaked with sweat, my mind was racing just knowing that the next breath I drew would create another major spasm. I saw the fear in my wife's eyes and in my stepdaughter, who was quite naturally upset. In one respect I was calm and trusting the Lord, but in another, my mind was tormented knowing I had to breathe again. Apparently my lungs were in respiratory arrest. It felt to me as though the ambulance took a long time getting to me, but in fact they arrived in just five minutes! The EMTs gave me a breathing treatment and loaded me into the van. I don't recollect much of the next week, in fact the only memory I have is being in ICU and being told that I was going to be put into a medically induced coma. I remember telling Lynn that I was very frightened.

When I woke up again … I thought I had been asleep for only three hours. Not so. It was three weeks later! But I could not move, I was totally paralyzed except for my right index finger. I'm fascinated at how calm I was and how peaceful my mind was. Perhaps the calm was due to the drugs I was being given, but more likely it was due to the multitude of corporate prayers that were being said on my behalf. From my perspective, faces would move in and out of my visual field very quickly. It was all very weird, I could not grasp what was going on. It took me a very long time to realize that I had, had a tracheotomy, which explained why I could not speak. When I finally realized I had a trachea, I communicated through my fear, that I did not like that on my throat!

I was asked to communicate by blinking once for yes

and twice for no. I could not do that! I fully understood what was being told to me, but I just could not blink my eyes on demand. Nothing anywhere on my body moved voluntarily, except my right index finger. It is stunning that my mind remained calm. I just seemed to accept the way I was. So strange looking back on that now, it is not my nature to be so accepting. I am also told that I was in a lot of pain but I have no memory of experiencing pain during the first several weeks.

I have vivid recollection, during the time I was comatose, of the doctor advising me that they had finally diagnosed my condition as H1N1, the swine flu. He also told me at that time that I was the first such diagnosed patient to be treated at Saratoga Hospital. I remember being very distressed when I heard that news and realized, at that moment, that I had nearly lost my life. Not being able to respond or move should have terrified me, but for some reason I was able to take it in stride. I had an unusual acceptance in the midst of all this, a genuine grace. Was my calmness the result of the work of the Comforter, the Holy Spirit? Was it a result of all the prayers that were being said for me? I have always taught that people who are too sick to pray for themselves, need others praying for them. I know that I was being carried on a tsunami of prayer!

A respiratory nurse told me that I could speak if I let her put her finger on my trachea. I do not like people putting their hands anywhere near my throat. Her offer frightened me and still does! But this nurse put her finger on the tube and I was able to say my first words in over three weeks. I looked into the eyes of my wife and said, "I love you" and wept buckets. Lynn wept also and so did the respiratory nurse. Though there was a deep sadness at that moment, there also was a serene sense of trust that everything was going to be alright eventually. My precious wife visited me daily from 8:00 a.m. until 8:00 p.m., for seventy-five days straight! It was, of course, exhausting for her but it was so comforting to have her by my side, even during the days I was not conscious of her presence. When I woke up three weeks later, I did not like it when she went home. I did not want to be without her, even though I knew that I was not alone.

Though I have no specific memory of people talking to me while I was comatose, I want to encourage you to please talk to those who you may know who are in a coma and cannot communicate with you. Tell them that you love them and encourage them to wake up and join you again. Though I cannot recall specific incidences of this happening to me, I know many others who do remember not just that someone spoke to them, but also what was said. Don't feel awkward. You can read to them, sing to them or simply carry on a one way conversation! Many of the hospital staff spoke to me once I could speak through the trachea. In fact many hospital personnel, even those not associated with my case, stopped by my room to ask how I felt and what it felt like to have the H1N1. Some people wanted to know why I thought I had it. But every one of them got the H1N1 inoculation after talking to me.

There has been a huge interest in whether I had a great mystical experience while I was comatose. Those who are curious have asked many questions about my time in the coma. Frequently asked questions are: "Did you see God?", "Did Jesus talk with you?", "What happened while you were close to death?", "Have you been given instructions for the rest of your life?" Virtually every question that has ever popped into your mind about such matters has been asked of me. You may remember that earlier in this book I shared about other instances where I came close to death, but I wrote of only one other instance where I had come this close previously. I am referring to the time that I drowned during a scuba dive off of Malta in 1975. I saw a yellow tunnel while I took in water, trying to breathe! Common to both of these near death experiences, was an amazing peace that followed my initial panic. But when I nearly drowned, I actually felt as though I had an option and I chose life. Thanks be to God! This coma was a very different experience because I had visions, very vivid and very real visions.

I remained hospitalized for nearly two months and upon release I went to a rehabilitation center. At rehab I was advised that some people who have been comatose may continue in the "reality" of their visions and dreams for some time after waking from the coma. I found that there were a couple occasions where I really had no idea what was going on due to the drugs I was being given. I was in and out of reality. For quite a while I simply could not comprehend what people were saying to me. Sometimes I saw moving jaws and heads coming and going, in and out of my awake visions. It all sounds very strange, but at the time—in my mind, it was quite normal! I have never used illicit drugs, but this may have been insight into such an experience. Another reason not to do drugs!

Another concern that followed the coma was that I might have sustained some brain damage due to a lack of oxygen. I am sure that a few of my dreams and visions were the cause of some alarm to those who visited. My visions seemed so real, like parallel realities. Sandra, who works closely with our ministry, appeared in one of my visions as a very kind short order cook! When I was eventually able to speak, during one of Sandra's visits, I asked her where she now lived (my vision of her as a short order cook took place in another location). I will always remember the look of grave concern on Sandra's face as she turned to look at Lynn and the doctor who were present! That was an instance of how I remained in a vision which had become my "reality". Such odd and awkward moments! Lynn told me later that before I could speak I would look at her and pucker my lips as if asking for a kiss. She teased that she hoped that I was puckering up because I had recognized *her*; and not because I was in the habit of doing that to all the nurses! Oh yes, one can even find humor in the darkness!

My dear brother, Alec, came from England to the USA twice while I was comatose. Sadly I have no memory whatsoever of his two visits. I did learn that he had poked me in the feet and told me to wake up during his visits. I cannot imagine what I would have felt if the roles were reversed and he had been in my shoes. I do so wish that I had been able to talk to him. I'm told that the medical monitoring equipment to which I was attached, registered positive improvement whenever I recognized familiar voices. So thank you Alec for taking part in my recovery. I feel certain that on a very deep level my brain recognized Alec as my brother and was comforted that he was physically present. My cousin, Virginia, a doctor who was living in New York at the time, also came to see me several times and was a terrific help to Lynn and Alec.

Initially I could not retrieve detailed memory of the visions and dreams I had. It took some time to recollect them as my mind was in a total muddle. It was funny because my confusion did not trouble me at all, it just seemed normal. Thank goodness! I am told that I was eventually given a drug to forget everything; I am so very glad about that. I am grateful not to remember what was done to me when I was comatose. I don't remember the tracheotomy or the feeding tube in my stomach, or the dialysis to save my kidneys and liver, or when both lungs were punched and drained of unwelcome fluid, or the ice blanket that covered me to lower my high fever, or the many blood transfusions. I was told all about these matters after the fact, but have no personal recall of them. The shunts, the needles, the constant care; Lynn and the nurses sitting full-time watching the dials of the respirator and the computers tasked with keeping me alive, each giving real time read outs and updates of what my lungs were doing, or not! Everything was being done to my body and I had no idea. But for those who were with me, especially my wife, these events are the sources of traumatic memories.

The visions and dreams I had during the coma took a while for me to remember, but when I did, they still seemed so very real. In time, I also began to realize that each vision had a Bible verse associated to it. Apart from one dream, each had very vivid colors and was extremely sharp in focus. These dreams and visions were so real, it was as if they had actually happened. I've had dreams in my life but these were very different.

The first vision I had was of floating in space. It was very dark, so dark that I could not see the earth. Slowly the stars became more and more vivid and bright. I was floating in a seated position as if in a gravity chair, just looking around. I was completely at peace. Strangely, it felt totally normal at the time. I've been known to sing David Bowie's song about Major Tom, *"Here am I floatin' 'round my tin can far above the world. Planet Earth is blue and there's nothing I can do."* There is nothing I can do! As I think about this now, it does make me a bit nervous. It was as though I was actually dead. Since then, this vision has been triggered by just looking at pictures of the stars in space. I was also triggered once when I walked the dog at night and looked up at the sky, I thought I was back in that gravity chair at that moment. Though this vision can trigger fear in me, the Bible verse I associate with it, gives me hope. After drowning in 1975, I had no fear of death. So I think that the fear attached to this vision is from being alone, not dead. I was totally alone. I have come to see this vision as part of our journey from earth to heaven. Jesus said, "Do not be afraid." and "I will never leave you or forsake you."

The actual Bible verse that I have connected to the first vision is from Matthew 4:16, *"The people living in darkness have seen a great light; on those living in the land of the shadow of death a light has dawned."* This verse makes sense of the vision to me. The next verse Matthew 4:17: *"From that time on Jesus began to preach, "Repent, for the kingdom of heaven has come near."* Oh my yes, the kingdom of heaven came very near. Indeed I was living in the shadow of death and I had definitely seen a great light. In Genesis 1:16, we are told: *"God made two great lights—the greater light to govern the day and the lesser light to govern the night. He also made the stars."* As I write this it is helping me clarify what I experienced during this harrowing time. I am having 20-20 hindsight at the moment. Had I been walking in darkness? Did God want me to see something in these visions? My prayer is that in time I will have deeper understanding, but currently I still have more questions than answers.

The second vision was of my house in heaven. I have written a bit of this one earlier in the book. There was great detail with such vivid colors in this vision. The first thing I saw was very green, healthy grass and a flower garden in front of my house with vivid red, perfect tulips. Beautiful! There were a few steps and then the house. Apparently I could walk, remember at the time I could not! The house was modern and made of glass, in a modular fashion in the shape of a diamond. The seams which secured the glass panes were made of steel, painted a high gloss red. I recall seeing a distinct number eight, painted white, on the door. Eerily, Lynn told me later that I'd been in ICU room number eight! How would I have known that? Interesting, that the number eight when turned on its side is the Infinity symbol. *It is a concept in many fields, most predominantly mathematics and physics, that refers to a quantity without bound or end. People have developed various ideas throughout history about the nature of infinity. The word comes from the Latin infinitas or "unboundedness".*[20] We have everlasting life in Christ!

The floor in my heavenly home was suspended and went out to the far corners of the diamond shape, in each room. Under the floor you could see water and in every room there was an eight inch section of floor missing where a gold chain was attached to a pure gold scoop for drinking the water beneath. That water was not just water it had to have been "Living Water". I can tell you that it tasted quite amazing, I remember thinking that I had never tasted anything so perfect, refreshing and satisfying. I noticed that there was no kitchen in my house in heaven, because the living waters that were provided were so fulfilling.

The Bible verse connected to this vision is from John 14:2 *"In my Father's house are many rooms; if it were not so, I would have told you. I am going there to prepare a place for you."* I believe that I saw the place that is prepared for me in heaven. It was very peaceful and "matter of fact;" serene and permanent. It felt right. It was well with my soul. But I was aware that Lynn was not there and I did not like that. From hindsight, I think the Lord allowed me to glimpse heaven, one of His mansions. I would be remiss not to also add this verse from John 4:14 here: *"But whoever drinks the water I give him will never thirst. Indeed, the water I give him will become in him a spring of water welling up to eternal life."* I pray that through Christ that living water may be poured out through ministry to others.

---

[20] http://en.wikipedia.org/wiki/Infinity

The third vision was of me waiting in a Victorian dining room. Once again the colors and sharp focus were distinct and unique. I was sitting at a walnut dining room table to the left of the carver seat. The place was perfect. The wallpaper was green and all the wood was deep dark walnut, another beautiful room in heaven. I was waiting. It took me some time to realize what or who I was waiting for as I looked around and admired the walnut carvings and a strange large cylinder above my head, covered in the same green wallpaper. It just did not make sense. I pondered this for a long time and then realized what it was. After my trip to Israel in 1998 I went to Lisieux, France and witnessed a leg bone of St. Therese on display. I have deep respect for St. Therese. This relic was in her basilica and it was encased in the same sized tube that was above my head in this vision. I knew St. Therese prays for priests, was she praying for me? I looked around some more and then I realized who I was waiting for…I was waiting for Jesus. I realized that I was waiting for Him to come into the room and greet me; to welcome me to heaven. He was going to give me the rules of living in heaven. Perhaps something about littering on the gold pavements? Again it was all very matter of a fact. There was no fear. Actually I was really looking forward to having a chat with the Lord. He did not come in. Then everything went blank. The Bible verse that seemed to attach itself to this vision is Luke 12:36: *"Like men waiting for their master to return from a wedding banquet, so that when he comes and knocks they can immediately open the door for him."* But there was no knock. The knock never came. It was not my time.

I had many other dreams and vision. Once I saw a beautiful pond and so many mansions, which connected by a small gauge train. The train was always waiting for you. I did not have to wait. I also became aware that other people were present, but I could not see them.

I puzzled over whether I was actually alone? In another vision I was going fishing. It was a large boat and we spent a lot of time being briefed about the dangers of fishing. This vision was all rather confusing, vivid like the others, but frightening. All that I could relate to this is the idea of being a "fisher of men." I was very aware of large sharp hooks, angry machinery and confusing computerized fish locators and weather predictors. This was an angry vision and most unsettling. Perhaps this vision was one where reality was breaking into my coma dreams because I've since learned that all around me there was the incessant sound of alarms and bells that kept going off in my hospital room as everyone was struggling to save my life. The Bible verse linked to this vision would be Mark 1:17: *"Come, follow me,"* Jesus said, *"and I will make you fishers of men."* Based upon my vision, perhaps we should attach this caveat to becoming fishers of men: it will not be easy and it will be confusing at times!

The most frightening vision was one of being in Sweden where they had government authorized euthanasia in my vision. In it, my funeral was to be held that Thursday at eleven o'clock in the morning, but I wasn't dead yet! In my vision I was on a gurney with green sheets and I could hear the clinking of champagne glasses in the next room as people were celebrating my life. I knew that the funeral was to be at eleven o'clock and I could see the clock which indicated that it was already ten-thirty. I saw my coffin was next to a ten by ten foot green killing table. I have no idea how I knew these things, much less how accurate I was, but I remember them clearly today. Then I watched as two male nurses came and took me off the table, very roughly. They put me on the killing table. As it was their job to kill me, they put their knees into my throat. I did not have the strength to stop them. This was a most terrorizing vision. After this vision, when I woke up, I did not want any male nurses anywhere near me for the rest of the stay at the hospital. Lynn has since told me that the tracheotomy was inserted at eleven o'clock in the morning! Now I wonder whether the clinking of champagne glasses in my vision was the clinking of the tools used to cut my throat. It is clear to me now that this vision occurred at the time of my tracheotomy and this is yet another good reason why I don't like anyone's hand anywhere near my throat!

The Bible verse that came to mind for this vision is John 5:21: *"For just as the Father raises the dead and gives them life, even so the Son gives life to whom he is pleased to give it."* An additional Bible verse that is reminiscent of this vision and which really gives me hope is from John 10:28: *"I give them eternal life, and they shall never perish; no one can snatch them out of my hand."*

The most comforting vision I had was of me crawling through a valley. I understood that this was the valley of the shadow of death as found in Psalm 23. Of course the scenery was so clear and beautiful. The greens were so green, the sky so blue. The rocks so steep and vivid. There was a well-worn path which I could not escape. There was no way off the path. It was clear that many had gone before me on this very same path. I looked and I saw a tableau of the three crosses on Good Friday. Jesus was looking at me from His cross. He was staring at me. His eyes were full of life, His body limp. I felt as though He was encouraging me. "You can do it Nigel" seemed to be His unspoken message. I then looked toward the other side of this valley, and there was that tableaux again. It kept moving to wherever I looked. Jesus was with me throughout this valley. I was in a commando crawl so familiar from my past. I was crawling through the valley of the shadow of death. I saw the shadow, it was the shadow of the crucifixion.

The Bible verse that comes to my mind in relation to

this vision is from 1 Peter 2:24 *"He himself bore our sins in his body on the tree, so that we might die to sins and live for righteousness; by his wounds you have been healed."* Of course, for obvious reasons, the other verse would be from Psalm 23:4 *"Even though I walk* (or crawl) *through the valley of the shadow of death, I will fear no evil, for you are with me; your rod and your staff, they comfort me.* For You Lord are with me… I am not alone.

It has taken me well over a full year to sort out these visions and even now, I am not sure I have a firm grasp on them. My sense is that these visions were the workings of God in my brain and soul. He was giving me hope, a hope for the future. He actually says that through the prophet Jeremiah 29:14: *"For I know the plans I have for you,"* declares the LORD, *"plans to prosper you and not to harm you, plans to give you hope and a future."*

I have no doubt that there was a huge battle going on for my soul during this time, but there was nothing I could to about it. I believe that something wanted me dead and those who worship that something were praying that I would die. I thank God for all those around the entire world who organized intercessors to continually lift me before the Lord for healing. I thank God for special saints like Beth Strickland, Torre Bissell, and The Rev. Canon Bob Haskell from the Episcopal Diocese of Albany, who got the word out about me daily, updating my healing needs each day for those who wanted to pray for me. The internet was an invaluable instrument in my healing. The website of the Diocese of Albany, within which my ministry resides, experienced an unparalleled increase of hits. Many logged onto diocesan blogs and prayed for me…it was overwhelming to read them following my discharge from the hospital. I could only read a few at a time. Such an outpouring of love and astounding demonstration of the power of corporate prayer.

I was carried on a stretcher of prayer just as the paralytic in the story from Mark 2:1-12. The key here is how powerful individual, mustard seed-sized faith prayer is when joined corporately with so many others. There was a huge and powerful radiation of prayer converging on my lungs which saved my life. The Bible exhorts us in 1 Thessalonians 5:16-18: *"Be joyful always; pray continually; give thanks in all circumstances, for this is God's will for you in Christ Jesus."*

I also learned that an Army unit in Baghdad was praying, a Marine unit in Afghanistan, as well as family and friends and thousands of others I did not even know. To be on the receiving end of such corporate prayer has been very humbling. If you prayed for me please accept a big THANK YOU. I hope you know how powerful your prayers were. My dear friend and mentor Francis MacNutt has always said, *"People are dying because people are not praying for them."* He is right. I know that your prayers saved my life. The Rev. Canon Andrew White, vicar of Baghdad, wrote about me in *Suffer the Children, Dispatches to and from the Front Line,* a book about children in war torn cities. He writes that when he needed people to pray he would ask the children of the church to pray as they seemed to be the most committed. On the last page of his book he writes, *"When an American friend of mine was critically ill recently, it was the children who came and prayed for him every day. And when he was discharged from hospital, we had a party."* I wept greatly when I read that, I was so deeply moved that children in war torn Baghdad were praying for me! To be on the receiving end of so many prayers is a very grand and overwhelming experience to say the least.

Many people wanted to visit me, however my wife very wisely blocked many. I am sorry if you were one of those blocked, but there were so many who came and Lynn was careful to guard my recovery. I am told that on one evening about thirty people came and held a prayer service for me in the lobby of the hospital. I was so moved to hear that. Many clergy also came to see me. One Sunday while I was in rehab, fifteen lined up outside my room! My very own "band of brothers." I am told that my bishop, The Rt. Rev. Bill Love, came to pray for me many times. He apparently would bend over me as he whispered his prayers into my ear, oftentimes kneeling beside my bed as he prayed. I am so deeply grateful to these saints who spoke healing prayers and prophetic words over me. My spiritual director, The Rev. Dr. Herbert Sanderson, a very wise man, continually quoted Isaiah 30:15 and it has stuck with me: *"In returning and rest you shall be saved; In quietness and confidence shall be your strength."* This verse literally carried me through my time in the ICU and in rehab. I clung to a silver cross with Jesus hanging on it, a gift from the former Bishop of Albany, the Rt. Rev. Dan Herzog, which now hangs over my desk. Jesus was in my hand during medical procedures and injections that I had. Whenever I felt pain, I tried to focus on Christ's wounds rather than my own.

I learned a great deal about the do's and don'ts of hospital visitation! Since I experienced this illness as the patient, I can now see what is helpful and what is not so helpful when visiting patients. One dear soul always stood at the head of my bed, just to the right—and I could not see him! I didn't have the strength to turn my head and whenever I tried, the trachea twisted in my throat and hurt me. Another visitor kept hitting the bed and every time I felt nauseous. Yet another sat on my bed. Please remember this one, do not sit on the bed of someone you visit in the hospital! Patients spend all their time in that bed and it is such a confined space that taking some of it away is rather intrusive and can be painful. Additionally, many people shouted at me as if I was deaf. I gently reminded them that I was not deaf. And still others shouted at me simply because I was in a wheelchair. It was quite a feat to finally be able to use a wheelchair, but the shouting was awful, even though I would remind people that I'm not deaf! Please don't shout at people in wheelchairs, we don't like it!

What people do while visiting patients is just amazing! Some folks I had to entertain… I did not like to do that. Some just sat and stared at me, perhaps practicing a holy presence or not knowing exactly what to say. That was better than those who gave me the clear impression that I needed to entertain *them*. Regardless of the quality of the visits, I have to say that I did not want to be alone. So even bad visits were better than no visits! I confess that this was a huge fear. I hated the hospital curtain to be drawn around me, I didn't want to be closed off or forgotten. Some visitors stayed too long and some left too soon. I actually prayed that some would go home, while there were others who I prayed would stay longer and pray some more for me! All my visitors prayed for me and that was very comforting. They would ask, as I have always taught, "How may I pray for you?" What worked best for me as a patient was accurate and targeted prayer. When people prayed, as the patient, I had the feeling of being surrounded in love and being brought before the Lord for His healing.

The one thing I wanted to talk about after coming out of the coma was the word: kindness. Everyone had been so kind. I felt that I was the recipient of an enormous outpouring of pure kindness. I remember telling Lynn quite urgently that I just wanted kind people in my life, that I just wanted to be surrounded by kind people. I wanted to keep the toxic people away until I was well enough to pray for them again. The nurses, the doctors and all those who cared for me: those who took my blood, who cleaned my room, who administered my meds—were all so kind. I liked that very much. It is such a good reminder for all of us to remember to practice kindness, it can make such a difference in our lives and the lives of others.

I remember the day I left Saratoga Hospital ICU. I was elated to be moving on in the healing process, but I also felt sadness to leave such an amazing team of people who had really cared for Lynn and me. Real and dear souls that went beyond the requirements of their jobs and worked as if they were privileged to serve their patients. It was not about a pay check. That staff did all their work with genuine compassion for their patients. I saw the Lord in all of the team that cared for me. An ambulance took me from the hospital to Sunnyview Rehabilitation Hospital. I noted my wife following in the car behind me. I WAS ALIVE! The trees had lost their leaves since early October and they were now bare. Snow now covered the ground, it was December. Where had autumn gone? Oh yes, I remember, I was out of this world! Apart from hospitalizations related to combat, I had last been in the hospital at age 6 when my tonsils were removed. Now, I had made a hospital my home for months! I was not only alive, but I was also taking with me valuable lessons to add to my ministry tool kit for visiting the sick in the future and continuing as a nursing home chaplain.

One of the many downsides of being unable to move for three months was the pressure wound that formed at the base of my spine. The pain and discomfort that it created was at times unbearable. While in rehab this wound had created a hole, 5/8 inch deep and big enough for two fingers to fit inside it, in my low back. The flesh had rotted away. I cannot begin to describe the pain, which interfered with my need to exercise in order to rehabilitate! Having been horizontal for so long I also had developed a major problem with my inner ear. Every time I tried to stand, it was such a huge effort. Since October, I had lost 53lbs and all of my muscle! Standing made me nauseous and I even vomited a few times. I just did not want to get up. I thought I would be horizontal for the rest of my life. After a few days, however, I was given sea sick pills and that worked. Being nauseous is awful, but not as bad as that pressure wound on my back.

Debridement is a medical term describing the removal of dead, damaged or infected tissue in order to improve the healing potential of remaining healthy tissue. When this procedure was done with a scalpel, I held onto the bed for dear life! I awoke the night following the procedure, thinking that I had wet the bed. I was cold and I felt a familiar feeling from when I was five years old! I remember feeling embarrassed as I went to push the call button for the nurse and finally overcame my reticence when I realized that they were likely used to this sort of thing. Giving myself permission to call for a nurse, I pulled out my right hand from under the sheets and saw that it was covered in blood. I then pulled back all the bed covers and saw that I was lying in a huge pool of blood. I pushed the call button. No one answered. I could not shout because of the trachea. I waited and prayed. Boy did I pray! There was a growing pool of blood all around me. I remained surprisingly calm because I knew that I was in the right place to have this happen—the hospital! But I could not get anyone to come to help me. After what seemed like an eternity had passed, a nurse showed up and immediately called for help from others. I soon had five nurses. They were just so amazing, calm and professional not making me panic. Looking back I'm surprised at how much peace I had while wondering if I might bleed to death from that gaping wound. But my prayers were answered, help arrived! I have so much respect for doctors and nurses, after this prolonged time in their care. Though I would not be here without the collective care of all of them, I encourage you to please look over my acknowledgements to praise God with me for some specific saints to whom I owe such a tremendous debt of gratitude.

Not to diminish all the good that I received while in their care, I did experience some things that generated concern in me whilst in the emergency room in rehab. I had such a bad pain in my side that it woke me up, so I was wheeled into the ER and asked many questions. The ER was very busy. There were people dealing with a gunshot wound and a heart attack. However, after I was pushed down a corridor, I was just left. With my oxygen equipment plugged into a wall outlet, unable to walk—I was left for seven and one-half hours! It had been four o'clock in the morning when I was wheeled to ER and now it was Noon. Struggling with the trachea, I could not speak loud enough and could not get help. I felt forgotten and shoved aside. Additionally, having been placed on a gurney with thin padding when I was rolled to the ER, I was suffering terrible pain! I was in acute agony and no one was helping me. "My God, My God, have You forsaken me?" I so rarely feel abandoned by God, but in my pain and frustration I cried out to Him. Looking back now, I believe a shift change may have created this unusual lack of care. After intense prayer, I remembered the words "Patient Advocate" and quietly asked someone to send me one. Within two minutes I was talking to one. Five minutes later I was being wheeled back to my room. If ever you have a similar concern in the hospital do not be afraid to use those words... Patient Advocate!

Note: *Off topic for one moment here, I am reminded that I learned from a doctor while I was there, that when a patient goes to the emergency room and says these words: "I do not feel safe at home," the staff will make every effort to keep you there.*

This illness produced more challenges to my faith than any other single event that I can recall at this time. A second time I thought God had abandoned me was when a plastic surgeon wanted to remove the pressure wound and graft skin from my thigh. He actually put two fingers in my wound without an anesthetic. Once again I am without words to tell you how incredibly painful that was. And I could not scream because of the trachea! The pain stayed with me for a full twenty-four hours. It was just excruciating. Even two nurses came to me, independently, and quietly told me that such treatment was cruel and that it should not have been done that way! After the second nurse left me, I wept for a long time. I just laid in the darkness and wept while I remained in so much pain. I thought of wounded combatants who must do the same when they have pain after a limb is removed. I tried to rationalize my feelings. I said out loud "Okay God, I was able to endure the horrors of H1N1 and now this? What gives? I have had enough! WHERE ARE YOU?" It was then that I was reminded of what I had taught time and again; that is, give thanks for the pain rather than fight it. As soon as I did that, the pain began to subside. Why had it taken me twenty-four hours to remember that?

Twice daily changing of the dressings for both the trachea and the pressure wound was another horrendous torment, especially the wet Q-Tip cleaning around the hole in my throat. Some nurses were very good at it and made it more tolerable, while others had less patience and added to the discomfort. I have to say my wife, Lynn, was just amazing at changing the dressings. (However, I still hate anyone putting a hand anywhere near my throat.) On top of all this, a wad of gauze had to be applied to my pressure wound, twice daily, to stop the wound from healing externally in advance of internal healing. The dressing had to be pulled out and then a new one stuffed into the hole! I prayed a lot during these procedures. I kept thinking how much pain our Lord was in from the nail wounds of His hands and feet and from the scourging of His body. Oh the pain, the indescribable pain. As I contemplated His pain, I wondered if He was giving me insight. I learned so much about the human condition and our need for healing.

Lynn and I have been back several times to the Saratoga Hospital ICU to say thank you and once to Sunnyview Rehabilitation Hospital. It is a long drive. The first time I went I was so surprised to see how small some of the nurses were. During my ordeal I saw them as well over six feet tall! I also remembered my room as much bigger than it was. Having a horizontal perspective on my surroundings certainly skewed my view. Returning was a moving experience. I wept going back to see those wonderful people who helped me through the valley of the shadow of death. They hugged me and wept with me, it was so humbling. I am told that not many former patients come back to the ICU to say thank you. This is a huge shout out to you, Ladies and Gents: Thank you all so very much for all that you did for me and all that you do for countless others!

Though patients naturally have trauma triggers associated with hospitalization, my wife endured much trauma as well. She stood by me for months, praying and hoping for my survival. We have learned that one identifiable trigger which evokes trauma memory for Lynn, is whenever I cough. Every time I cough, she is instantly transported back in her mind to October 10, 2009. I now also know that, on October 23, 2009, I nearly died. That day, I was still in a coma and the readings on the computers were not looking good. I was on 100% oxygen. The doctors advised that they had done all they could for me, they prepared those around me for the worst. I have no memory about that time. Most likely I was in that Victorian dining room, in the heavenlies, waiting for Jesus. Not remembering any of this and believing that God was giving me visions and dreams in unfathomable detail on that very day, warms my heart. But it is unimaginable what those who were waiting and praying for me were thinking and feeling.

One residual byproduct from this battle for my life, is my need to learn not to panic when I am out of breath. As of this writing I have been told by my doctors that I have lost thirty five percent of my lung capacity. I have been cautioned over and over again in rehab to slow down. Take time to stop and smell the roses. Breathe without panicking. I still am guilty of forgetting this when trying to climb the stairs. Half way up the stairs, time and again, I must stop and practice breathing. But in hindsight, this is such an improvement. I recall that when I first came home, just before Christmas 2009, I could barely maneuver the first step of our stairs.

In addition to having been made aware of the rare, but occasional lack of kindness in the care provided in a hospital setting, I now also see the downside of the less than charitable manner with which some of humankind treats people with disabilities. All of this has been an incredible learning experience for me and I am quite certain that it will fuel even greater compassion within me. But I am just amazed at how many inconsiderate people park in disabled parking spaces without the correct stickers or markers. I find that really sad. I had never noticed that before and I have to say that it now really ticks me off. I discussed, with one of the physical therapists at a local rehab center in Greenwich NY, the fact that no one can see the disability in me because it is in my lungs. To strangers, I appear to walk fairly normally. My disability is that I do not have the energy or capacity to go far because of my lung restriction. I never imagined how slow the healing process would be from this illness. And, of course, I've had to reckon with the fact that I am not the same man I was before I was sick. A friend very kindly gave me a rowing machine in order to help me get fit again. The first time I sat on it I realized that I could not use it when I could not get up from it. I was stuck! I slowly crawled to a nearby chair and as I imagine an iguana might, I very slowly crept up the chair to bring myself to a stand again. It is a long road to recovery, but I am alive thanks be to God! My prayer now is, of course, tongue in cheek, "Oh God, give me patience and give it to me now!"

What happens after the healing? There are not many references in the Bible to what happened, afterwards, to those who were healed by Jesus. We do know that King Hezekiah was given fifteen more years of life after the Lord said, "I have seen your tears, I have heard your prayers, I will heal you." But we know nothing of what happened to him in those fifteen years. The blind men and the lepers, those who begged for a living, all those who asked were healed…but what happened to them after their healing? We only know that one of the ten lepers, who was healed of their leprosy, even came back to say thank You to Jesus. In the emotional and spiritual healing of Mary Magdalene, we know that she became a valued member of the community later on, but not much else. So as I contemplate His gift of healing to me, my spiritual mind has been struggling with how to "be" after this ordeal. In addition to my enormous gratitude for being alive, my illness has created times of extreme stress, particularly in my being uncertain how I am to live now that I am well. I am still a work in progress, as my heart, mind and soul continue to sort this all out together.

One last sweet moment that I savor. While I was still in ICU, Beth Strickland, Deployment Officer for the Diocese of Albany published the email address of the hospital on the diocesan website. One day a hospital secretary delivered to my room a full ream of emails that they had been printed out. She apologized that they'd run out of color ink. She handed me the ream, but I couldn't hold it. She put it by my bed. Then on her way out she stopped and, pausing to look at me, asked, "Who are you?" I smiled and replied, "I suppose that I am a man who is loved." The tears flowed freely down my face. In John 15:12 Jesus is recorded as having said: *"Love one another as I have loved you."* I have experienced that love. I will be forever grateful for all the love that I received and all the prayers that were said on my behalf. I am convinced that my life was saved as a result of prayer. Thanks be to God!

CHAPTER TWENTY

The 911 Emergency List

"The Solution Is Life on God's Terms: With the arrival of Jesus, the Messiah, that fateful dilemma is resolved. Those who enter into Christ's being-here-for-us no longer have to live under a continuous, low-lying black cloud. A new power is in operation. The Spirit of life in Christ, like a strong wind, has magnificently cleared the air, freeing you from a fated lifetime of brutal tyranny at the hands of sin and death."

Romans 8:1-2 (The Message)

*"But seek ye first the kingdom of God,
and his righteousness; and all these things
shall be added unto you"*

Matthew 6:33
(King James Version)

When we have an emergency and we dial 9-1-1, the Operator may respond by asking what service is needed: fire, police or ambulance? Or the Operator may ask us, "What is the nature of your emergency?" If, for example, we are a pregnant woman who is about to give birth; after dispatching the correct service on the computer screen, the Operator will then reach for a flip chart which will prompt her or him to ask the appropriate question, for example, "Is the patient breathing?" Per that flip chart, instructions will continue to be given to that mother up to and after the birth of the baby. Step by step instructions will be provided which clearly spell out what must be done.

Hopefully, the emergency service that was dispatched will have arrived before the end of those instructions.

We know that some people are prone to slipping into serious negativity in their minds such as depression, rejection, or even switching alters/personalities in the case of someone struggling with Dissociative Identity Disorder (DID). When that negativity arises in us we may beat ourselves up emotionally, we might switch off, zone out, stare off into space, etc. When we are feeling good about ourselves and feel as though we are in our sound minds, it could be a really good time to create our own 9-1-1 flip chart, a preemptive set of instructions that can help us avoid drowning in our negativity. We can write our own emergency list that can help us whenever those negative reactions are triggered in everyday life. So when we are triggered and find ourselves slipping into that familiar, but dark place; we can pull out our 9-1-1 Emergency List and help restore ourselves to the present moment without the usual trauma response. This list must be, by its nature, very personal to each of us, individually.

So what works for you? Think this through carefully and then write your own list so that you will have something that can quickly turn a tidal wave of negative thinking away from you. When you finish your list, laminate it and keep it in your purse or wallet. Here are some ideas to include when making your own 9-1-1 Emergency List:

1.) Pray and ask for help from the Lord to know what will most effectively defuse your trigger response. Jesus told us in John 16:24: *"Until now you have not asked for anything in my name. Ask and you will receive, and your joy will be complete."* Again in Luke 11:10, Jesus said: *"For everyone who asks receives; he who seeks finds; and to him who knocks, the door will be opened."*

2.) Find a Bible verse that really speaks to your need. If you have internet access, go to: www.biblegateway. com for ideas. Just enter a word that is on your mind in their keyword search and read all the verses that contain that word.

3.) Go to a "safe place" in your mind or even go there physically. Think about something that warms your heart or actually go to a place where the view is uplifting to you or just somewhere that you enjoy.

4.) Call a friend, pastor, therapist or healing minister who can help you.

5.) Make a cup of tea, read a book, watch Christian broadcasting on television, write a letter to someone.

6.) Exercise, meditate, play with your pet, go for a walk, take some deep breaths.

Incorporate your own ideas as you expand on your personal list. Just know that your goal is to list alternative ways in which you can bring yourself back into the present moment without loitering in the stress of the trauma. Seek first the kingdom of God and I believe that the Lord will inspire you to come up with a comprehensive list that can make all the difference in your ability to cope in the future.

You may recall that I shared earlier in this book how the Lord divinely stopped obsessive depressive thinking on my part. He often uses pictures when He inspires me, and this was one of those. I think of it as a Christian Prescription. I liken depression to looking down a tube that goes to the center of the earth. The tube is painted black and there is a spiral channel attached to the side wall. A dark ball is released whenever we go into our depression mode. The ball gathers momentum in the tube as it goes deeper and deeper into Hell. In time, the hand of Jesus repeatedly stops that ball, each time closer and closer to the release point—until that ball, when released, is stopped immediately by Christ's own hand!

Jesus is the Healer and He does not wants us to slide into those familiar places of darkness in our minds. Consider thinking about the Christian Prescription above and seeing the Hand of God prevent you from spiraling into the abyss. Meanwhile, spend some time thinking on what your 9-1-1 Emergency List should contain. The Lord knows you better than anyone, even yourself. So take some time and seek His counsel relative to your list. He would never withhold from you any gift that would help heal your mind, heart, body, soul and spirit. So go on and ask Him to help you make your list and then carry it with you at all times, reminding yourself that He has already given you a path of escape.

Know that you are never alone. Know that He will never forsake you. Know that He understands you and what you need better than anyone else ever will. Now read and be encouraged by this passage from 1 Corinthians 10:13 (New Living Translation): *"The temptations in your life are no different from what others experience. And God is faithful. He will not allow the temptation to be more than you can stand. When you are tempted, he will show you a way out so that you can endure."*

Chapter Twenty-One

A Life Plan: Seven Steps to Godly Alignment

"'For I know the plans I have for you,' declares the Lord, 'plans to prosper you and not to harm you. Plans to give you a hope and a future.'"
Jeremiah 29:11

"Be joyful always; pray continually; give thanks in all circumstances, for this is God's will for you in Christ Jesus."
1 Thessalonians 5:16-18

"Do not conform any longer to the pattern of this world, but be transformed by the renewing of your mind. Then you will be able to test and approve what God's will is his good, pleasing and perfect will."
Romans 12:2

I am writing this in 2011. We are in some very tough economic and politically tumultuous times and we must really trust in the Lord if we are going to experience any peace. Just like a car that needs to have its front wheels aligned, we need to align our lives with God and with one another. If one of your tires is pulling one way while another is pulling in yet another direction, we are going to rip the tread off those tires. In the same way, we should seek to avoid stressing our relationship with God and each other. Here are seven steps that I would suggest for Godly alignment:

1) Spend a minimum of twenty minutes (very likely you'll want to spend more) writing down everything you would like to accomplish in your life. Think outside of the box. In doing this exercise do not allow finances, circumstances or geographic location to influence what you do or don't include on this list. In fact, there should be no blocks or obstacles in this exercise. Just write down everything you would like to do! This list is not cast in stone, it can be added to or subtracted from. It is totally flexible and adaptable. If you are married, you may spend time making your lists in one another's presence, but don't exchange your information and discuss them together…just yet.

2) Once you have finished your list, review it carefully and then choose your top five and put them in order of their priority for you.

3) If you are married, once you have prioritized your top five items, it's time to go over your lists together. Have fun with this, avoid looking for offense based upon what your spouse has included or failed to include on their list. Perhaps you will learn something about your spouse that you didn't know or that you had forgotten! As you compare your lists, look for goals or desires you have in common— wherever your loose threads can be woven together. Remember this wasn't meant to be practical. There are no right or wrong answers!

4) Now lift up your lists to the Lord, praying along these lines: "Lord, this is what I/we would like to do with our lives, what do You think? I/we want to align myself/ourselves with You, knowing that

You have given me/us the gift of free will. Into Your hands I commend my life as I try less and trust more in You. I stand on Your word in Jeremiah 29:11-14: *"For I know the plans I have for you," declares the Lord, "Plans to prosper you and not to harm you. Plans to give you a hope and a future. Then you will call upon me and come and pray to me, and I will listen to you. You will seek me and find me when you seek me with all your heart. I will be found by you."* Make any revisions or clarifications that the Lord may show you in response to your prayer.

5) Take your completed "Life Plan", fold it and place it in your Bible. Leave it with the Lord.

6) Be proactive in your life journey and do not let others hinder you or put you down. Seek harmony and understanding as you share your life plan with your spouse. I do not suggest sharing it with others…just with your spouse and with God.

7) Do not sit back and expect your top five to somehow land in your lap. Engage. Be proactive. Enter in and live your life. Jesus Christ died that we might live and have life abundant. LIVE YOUR LIFE to the fullest. No excuses!

CHAPTER TWENTY-TWO

Seven Steps toward Victory in the Battlefield of Life

A bruised reed he will not break,
and a smoldering wick he will not snuff out,
till he leads justice to victory.
Matthew 12:20

Drawing upon my own personal healing experiences as well as the healing journeys of others I have been privileged to accompany over the last twenty some years; I compiled a list of specific actions or attitudes which will amplify the healing process in our lives. Of course, there are any number of things we could list that would augment our healing. I confess that I was up to thirty-five suggestions on my list before I realized that I needed to narrow my focus! As I refocused, I chose to edit my growing list to include only those things that I knew had been victorious in helping me and others heal from past emotional and physical wounds. I arrived at seven. Biblically speaking seven is the number assigned to perfection and/or completion. When I asked myself and God what had really helped me and others to heal, quite wonderfully my list was narrowed to seven steps!

These seven steps are:

1. Pray. Ask and communicate your need to God and others.

2. Forgive yourself. Forgive others. Ask God to forgive

you and the others,

3. Seek healing for the past. Be proactive in getting help. Doctors, nurses, pastors, therapists, healing ministers and medications are generally on your side.

4. Do not give the perpetrator any power over you.

5. Live in, and enjoy, the present moment.

6. Take a look at your life in the shape of a pie chart.

a) What can you change?

b) What can God change?

7. Have fun!

Let's take a look at each of these steps, one at a time:

1. Pray. Ask and communicate your needs to God and others.

Personal prayer, as well as the power of corporate prayer (others praying for you), has definitely brought me through the valley of the shadow of death. Prayer is a solid investment in your future. Whenever we pray, something in us changes. Though our prayers may not change others, something shifts within us as we are brought closer to the source of all healing…none other than the Lord Himself! Jesus told us to "Ask." We need to ask Him. We need to communicate our needs to God. Remember that something always happens whenever we pray. God's answer to prayer is either 'yes', 'no', or 'not yet'. Please do not limit God in your prayers. Go on now, get on your knees, either alone or together with your spouse, and pray. Then be on the lookout for what happens.

2. Forgive yourself. Forgive others. Ask God to forgive you and the others.

This perhaps is the most difficult thing for a human being to do. Why should we forgive? The real problem with unforgiveness is that in holding onto it, we allow the perpetrator to continue their crime. Forgiveness is a decision to put the perpetrator behind us, so that we can move forward. By forgiving the perpetrator, we're not letting them off the hook. No, instead we are putting a stop to the spread of emotional cancer and its further eating away of our souls. We can put a stop to the spread of bitterness and resentment and the ultimate theft of our joy and our ability to live life abundantly. Oh God, help forgive us our trespasses as You forgive us our trespasses; and help us forgive those who trespass against us as You forgive those who trespass against us!

The Rev. Brennan Manning, Ret. USMC, in his book, *Abba's Child: The Cry of the Heart for Human Belonging*, is quoted: *"When I allow God to liberate me from unhealthy dependence on people, I listen more attentively, love more unselfishly, and am more compassionate and playful. I take myself less seriously, become aware that the breath of the Father is on my face and that my countenance is bright with laughter in the midst of an adventure I thoroughly enjoy."*[21]

---

[21] ©1994, 2002 NavPress Colorado Springs, CO

3. Seek healing for the past. Be proactive in getting help. Doctors, nurses, pastors, therapists, healing ministers and medications are generally on your side.

Sadly I meet with many people who are disenchanted with their doctor or therapist. They often dump their concerns on me about the lack of bedside manner of those who are supposed to be helping them heal. I often remind them that the professionals they see are part of their healing team, even when they may be having a bad day. Many long term patients share stories where I can understand why they may feel irritated and may even experience more cause for pain. Therefore I recommend that the patient, counselee or supplicant, be proactive! Ask for help. Ask for clarification. Using words like, "Can you please help me understand?" can go a long way in keeping a healthy relationship with the person you have chosen to come alongside you in your healing journey. Even though you may only have seven minutes with your doctor or you may be limited to 50 minutes with your therapist, make the most of the time you have. One way you can maximize your time together is to write down what your needs are before your appointment. Then take your notes with you so that you do not leave unheard, confused, or dissatisfied.

4. Do not give the perpetrator any power over you.

Sadly I see so many people who hang onto the "offense" or "horror" that resulted from what someone did to them in the past. The wounded one, the one who was the victim, can hold onto their hurt like a pit bull with a bone. As you would expect, if you dared put your hand anywhere near that bone, a pit bull may end up with your hand as well as that bone! So it is, sometimes, with those who have been wounded and who become embittered over what someone did to them in the past. They bite! Yet, no perpetrator of your past wound can continue to hurt you unless you give them power over you. I refer you back to number two on this list! Even if the perpetrator of your wound is dead, they are still hurting you from beyond the grave when you are tethered to them by your unforgiveness. In order to heal, you must be set free from your bitterness and your lack of forgiveness toward others. And sometimes the one who you really need to forgive is *you*! Ask the Lord, He'll show you if that is true in your case.

In Mark 11:25, Jesus is quoted as saying, *"And when you stand praying, if you hold anything against anyone, forgive him, so that your Father in heaven may forgive you your sins."* Finally if you're thinking that the New Testament is the only place that asserts God's ultimate authority over all, take a look at this passage from I Chronicles 29:11 in the Old Testament: *"Yours, O LORD, is the greatness and the power and the glory and the majesty and the splendor, for everything in heaven and earth is yours. Yours, O LORD, is the kingdom; you are exalted as head over all."* Wow! Now consider that in the closing sentence of the Lord's Prayer, most Protestant churches use words comparable to these: "For yours is the kingdom and the power and the glory for ever and ever. Amen." As you read both the passage from 1 Chronicles 29:11 and the closing words of the Lord's Prayer, notice that there is no mention of anyone else's or anything else's power, just the power of God! So why would you give power to those who have sinned against you? Take a moment and ask yourself what is holding you captive? What's keeping you far off from your healing? Certainly not your God!

5. Live in, and enjoy, the present moment.

If we allow the past to control our present we run smack into our problems. Of course the past molds us into who we are today, but if we live in the past we are not really living. Instead, we are reminiscing, lamenting, and continually revisiting all the "could've, would've, should've" scenarios which can do nothing to change our past or enhance the present. Is it a coincidence that the word "present" refers to an actual point in time (this very moment) in addition to meaning "a gift?" To find the gift of being content in the moment, you need not escape your daily reality. Seeking and asking for peace in the present moment can be so powerful and such a gift to your soul. Try to actively live in the present moment and enjoy what you see. Additionally, when we try to skip over the present moment and rush ahead to what we hope will be a better tomorrow, we lose the precious "gift" of the present and miss the enjoyment that God intends for us. *"Therefore I tell you, do not worry about your life, what you will eat or drink; or about your body, what you will wear. Is not life more important than food, and the body more important than clothes? Look at the birds of the air...your heavenly Father feeds them. Are you not much more valuable than they? Who of you by worrying can add a single hour to his life? "And why do you worry about clothes? See how the lilies of the field grow....If that is how God clothes the grass of the field...will he not much more clothe you,...So do not worry...do not worry about tomorrow, for tomorrow will worry about itself..."* Matthew 6:25-34

6. Take a look at your life in the shape of a pie chart.

a) What can you change?
b) What can God change?

Take a few minutes now and try to draw your life in the shape of a pie chart. Draw it as it is at this present moment, right now. Work out, percentage wise, how much time you spend in the following pursuits: eating, sleeping, working, playing, hobbies, computer, email, cooking, cleaning, driving, sports, watching television, talking on the phone, talking to others one on one, etc. How much time do you spend just thinking? How much time do you spend somewhere other than home? How much time do you devote to prayer; or saying 'thank you' or appreciating others? Take a thorough look at where your time goes? Now with that done, have a look at what you can change. What do you have control over? Ask yourself what you might need to change in order for you to live life in greater alignment with God and in pursuit of His peace. Then look at what changes you could make with God's help.

Now redraw your pie chart the way you would like it to be. Put your new pie chart where you can see it every day. Pray and ask the Lord to rearrange your life the way you and He both would like it to be. This is not an easy task and it may take a few "drawings" to get it right but do persevere. To glimpse your life this way can be transformational to you and those who love you. If you are married try doing this together, you may both learn valuable information about one another and for one another's future well-being.

7. Have fun!

You want a bottom line? Well, here it is: Have fun!

In walking out these steps, you may find yourself in an unfamiliar place—you may enter into a place of joy and peace! You might actually begin to see the colors of the flowers and the expression in people's eyes as you pass by. You may regain your self-confidence that allows you to look into the eyes of the people in your life and to truly see them. Just last night I got to look into the eyes of a woman who has just learned that she has been healed of cancer. What I saw in her eyes made me weep. Her entire face has been transformed since the week before; indeed, since I first met her months ago. Her healing was visible in her countenance and through her eyes. Not only was her cancer healed, but so has her soul been healed!

Have fun, not at others' expense you understand, but treat your soul to some fun. Pray and ask the Lord to help you in your quest for joy and see what happens. He will delight your heart! Seek first the Kingdom of God and all these things will be added to you. Ask for His gift of joy and pay attention as He fulfills your prayer.

Please do not mistake what I am saying here. I am not prescribing a formula. I am imparting to you the top seven steps that have helped me, and countless others, to win on the battlefield of life. Healing is a process, a journey. The goal is wholeness and the ability to truly accomplish what Jesus came to insure that you would have—life in abundance.

I pray that you will think a while on what I have written here and that these steps may inspire you to think and act differently. I pray that you might reach out for your healing as the Lord offers it to you. I pray that you will begin to walk on a new path, one that leads to life everlasting and not a dead-end. I pray that you will allow the Lord to help you move from rejection, depression and the pain of your traumas into a new place of peace as you accept His invitation to live a life only He can make available to you.

Please read this selection from 2 Corinthians 5:16-20 (The Message): "...*Now we look inside, and what we see is that anyone united with the Messiah gets a fresh start, is created new. The old life is gone; a new life burgeons! Look at it! All this comes from the God who settled the relationship between us and him, and then called us to settle our relationships with each other. God put the world square with himself through the Messiah, giving the world a fresh start by offering forgiveness of sins...We're speaking for Christ himself now: Become friends with God; he's already a friend with you.*" And I say a hearty "Amen!" to that.

CHAPTER TWENTY-THREE

Welcome Home

Now it had happened as they were coming home, when David was returning from the slaughter of the Philistine (Goliath), that the women had come out of all the cities of Israel, singing and dancing, to meet King Saul, with tambourines, with joy, and with musical instruments.

1 Samuel 18:6

*And Saul also went home to Gibeah;
and valiant men went with him,
whose hearts God had touched.*

1 Samuel 10:26

"Welcome home!" is a greeting that has become synonymous with combat veterans returning from tours of active duty. These veterans are comprised of men and women who have been affected in some way by their combat experience. Some were wounded physically; others, emotionally; while yet others were wounded both physically and emotionally. Their lives may have been changed by just one tour of duty or, in the case of one of my friends, fourteen tours of duty! What impact does their service have on their minds? What impact does their service have upon their relationships? The fallout from combat can be traumatic, in itself, as veterans return home to what was once normal life. Confronted with their trauma experiences in the familiar of what was formerly "home", yet another war is created for them—this one within their own minds.

Many of these veterans desperately try to hang onto their sanity. The Bible seems to address this issue as well. Take a look at 2 Chronicles 25:10 with me: *"So Amaziah discharged the troops that had come to him from Ephraim, to go back home. Therefore their anger was greatly aroused against Judah, and they returned home in great anger."* Anger is just one of many emotions that may be triggered in veterans who have been traumatized. They struggle as they attempt to re-enter the stream of life that was once their norm.

Knowing how difficult it is for these men and women to fit in again makes the small graces that they sometimes experience, all the sweeter. I'm referring to how wonderful it is when unexpected expressions of gratitude are bestowed upon returning veterans. It's so endearing when complete strangers signal their gratitude to uniformed military personnel who happen to be walking in a public place, such as an airport. It's just heartwarming. I've witnessed smiling men and women lift their right hands, palm side up, placing them over their hearts and then extending their hands forward, gesturing toward the veteran, as if to say, "Thank you from the bottom of my heart for your service." Those are powerful unspoken demonstrations of thankfulness, publicly "stated" with a compassionate smile. Such a small gesture has such major consequences for the veterans.

Not once in thirty years did I ever hear either of those two greetings, "Welcome Home" or "Thank you"! It can make a huge difference to hear just one person in your life say those words. Eventually, that one person was The Rt. Rev. Harold Miller who said "Thank you" to me and changed my life! Those words positively stunned me. My eyes opened wide like one who is seeing something shocking for the first time, as I realized that out of the blue in a place I would never have expected, I heard someone actually say 'thank you' and really mean it. My soul and spirit responded to those two little words as though a giant flame was warming my heart with hope. After thirty years someone actually thanked me for serving in the military! And it was said and directed to me, specifically! I believe it was at that moment, that the Welcome Home Initiative was birthed. If hearing those two words meant so much to me, what about all those other veterans who were quietly suffering? The words, "Thank you," were dormant triggers for me, like a flower seed in a packet waiting to be planted and germinated. Such a blessing!

It is interesting how often overworked phrases can suddenly dive bomb into our hearts and make us see and hear what we should know, but which had escaped us. For instance, since we are looking at the power of two little words, I am reminded how much my life was changed when Dr. Francis MacNutt challenged me to "have fun!" Francis will turn 86 years old this year and he has never stopped "having fun" ministering, sharing and teaching the healing gifts of Jesus Christ. Then there were the two words spoken by my own father, The Rev. David Mumford, who said "be available" which have also had a huge impact on my life. Over the years it is clear to me that if I just remain willing and available, God can use me to His glory. Finally, the person who first said "Welcome Home" to me, was the Rt. Rev. David Bena, also known fondly as Bishop Dave. He said that to me at the end of the first Welcome Home Initiative retreat we did together. Those words went straight to my heart and soul. Someone had actually said "Welcome Home" to me and suddenly things started to make sense. I had bottled up all this war stuff, stored it in my mind all locked up—or so I thought. That "stuff" had affected my heart and my soul every day of my life. It had prevented me from living my own life to the fullest. It was a mill stone around my neck that was trying to drag me under. The aftermath, the stigma, the shame, the emotional pain that was secretly tucked away, was now exposed. My combat trauma dated back to 1971 and it is now 2011. Is forty years an uncommon length of time to carry this "stuff?" Very sadly, no.

I vaguely remember coming home from the hospital in1977 after being diagnosed with Shell Shock. But I vividly remember coming home from the hospital on December 23, 2009, after my bout with H1N1. We pulled into the garage and I slowly got out of the car, in much pain from the pressure wound on my back. I moved in slow motion up the three steps into the kitchen, pausing at each step to catch my breath. I shuffled to the entrance hall, where I just fell apart emotionally. The splendid, overwhelming joy of being home was grossly marred by the realization that I was not the man I was when I left in that ambulance three months earlier. How many servicemen have that exact same kind of homecoming? How many are in extraordinary pain in their minds and/or bodies due to the loss of a limb or bearing other visible scars from an IED?

In both homecomings I was a broken man. Broken by combat the first time. Broken by physical disease the second time. My mind and body had taken a beating both times. "Welcome home" are two red carpet words which also serve to have a sobering effect. Coming home causes us to see clearly what has changed. Coming home ushers in a time to supposedly convalesce but it is more likely to become a time to lick the wounds and let the dust settle. Convalescing was unfamiliar to someone like me. I am not good at it! What type A personality would be good at it? How do you bring the go-go-go; get-it-done personality to a stop? In rehab, I tried to make that alpha aspect of my personality work for me as I tried to recover, but then my lungs wouldn't't cooperate to allow me to complete the required exercises. My lungs became a brick wall of resistance upon my homecoming in

2009. Whereas, the wall I had hit in my 1977 post-combat homecoming had been my self-confidence which had been shattered in combat. Gone; my confidence just flew away!

I found out, over a year later, that blood had pooled in my legs and that my skin color had been vivid purple with white blotches. I learned that my kidney and liver had been shutting down and that I had been on the close down journey into death. I am told that these events indicate that I was medically within one to three hours of death. I did not know, for a very long time, that I had come so close to death. It was shocking, but also an amazing revelation. Now I understand why the doctor said to me, "Nigel, I have never seen anyone as close to death without dying as you were." LORD, You brought me to the brink of death, thank You for bringing me out of the valley of the shadow of death.

Of course, this brings me back to the question that has returned to me many times since I escaped death in combat in the 1970's and again following H1N1 in 2009. Of course, that question is: Okay, now what?

Having survived two such ordeals in my life, I am a very grateful man. I am thankful to be alive; thankful for all the prayers that were said for me; thankful to God and all those unnamed people who prayed for my life to be spared, most of whom I will never know. Thank you. Thank You, God. Thank You, Jesus. Thank You, Holy Spirit.

The following verse found in Daniel 6:10 sums up the feelings I have in completing this book: *"Now when Daniel knew that the writing was signed, he went home. And in his upper room, with his windows open toward Jerusalem, he knelt, as was his custom, down on his knees three times that day, and prayed and gave thanks before his God."*

I'm now heading upstairs to my "upper room," where I am going to open the windows that face east. I'm going to get on my knees and I'm going to, again, say aloud again to God and to the thousands or more who lowered me, the paralytic (at the time), on the stretchers of their prayers, through the roof for Jesus to heal. THANK YOU!

Be well, do good works and for the sake of God, love one another.

WELCOME HOME!

CHAPTER TWENTY-FOUR

The Prayers

*"He sent them out to proclaim the kingdom
of God and to heal the sick."*
Luke 9:2

*"Rejoice always, pray continually, give thanks
in all circumstances; for this is God's will
for you in Christ Jesus."*
1 Thessalonians 5:16-18

A Prayer for the Spouse of a Combatant

Lord Jesus, thank you for bringing my loved one home.
Please give me patience and understanding,
*Help me appreciate my loved one and be compassionate
about things*
Seen and unseen.
*Help me to let go where I need to let go and help me to
love and*
Forgive where I need to love and forgive.
*Help me communicate without walking on thin ice and
when*
*Buttons are pushed help me to understand what is going
on in the*
Mind of my loved one.
*Please give me wisdom and the right words to defuse
any verbal bombs.*

Help me to welcome my loved one home and, as the dust
settles, and the daily routines come into play, help me in
the moment.
Lord, I know not what is going on in my loved one's
mind, I have a rough
Idea what he or she has gone through but I really do not
know
How to help him or her except by being there and loving.
Help me to love, nurture and draw closer and not to
Let "the war" stand in between us.
Please help me to remember we are on the same side and
that the enemy is far away
but that some of the war has infected our household.
Jesus we invite your peace, love and compassion into our
house.
Lord if the enemy tries to break us PLEASE stand
between us and heal us.
Help me to love the person you have given me even if
they have been
So changed by combat.
Please give me a nurturing, forgiving and understanding
heart so the war is over there
and not in my kitchen!
Amen.

A Prayer for the Caregiver of a Traumatized Patient

Lord Jesus help me to come alongside my patient.
Help me try to understand in the present moment that
He or she is still in combat within their mind.
Help me help them in the tension of the transition.

Help them understand that I am not the enemy and that
I am on their side.
I pray for wisdom when I am pushed away or rejected in
anyway
When my patient is in combat mode.
I pray for Godly rewiring of the brain in any damage
that may have
Taken place either from the shock waves of a bomb or
In the "play back" of the horrific memories that I do not
understand.
Jesus please give me the gift of healing to help my
charge.
Please give me the gift of wisdom in when to speak and
what to speak
And to be silent when needed.
Thank you God for the privilege of putting me in this
position.
Amen.

A Prayer for the Parents of a Combatant

Lord Jesus please help me.
I am so honored that my son/daughter has served my
country but my
Heart is so torn. I know that you will never leave me or
forsake me.
Please never leave or forsake my son/daughter. Protect,
sanctify, and be with him/her that they may be under
the shadow of your wings. Help me as I pray for their
protection, preservation and safe homecoming.
Jesus help me to really pray and to understand that you
are with me and that you will never let me go.

Take my hand in the fear, in the unease and strengthen
my soul with your love.
Until we meet again.
Help me to love unconditionally upon their return.
Amen.

A Prayer for the Victims of Abuse

Oh God my soul weeps.
I try to understand your free will but I do not
Understand man's inhumanity to man.
I have been so traumatized, so wounded, so hurt
how can I forgive?
How can I live my life after such horrors.
Teach me oh God to love and trust again.
Teach me how to live, not as a victim but as a healed
And strengthened person whom you love so much.
Heal my soul Jesus.
Heal the very wound that is within me.
By Your stripes I am healed, by your wounds I am
healed.
Help me to find the right therapist and the right team
To help me regain the years the locusts have eaten.
Father forgive them, they did not know what they were
doing.
Please help me.
Amen.

A Prayer for a Sufferer of PTS

Oh God what is going on in my mind?

I have seen too much, I have experienced such a trauma
Please help me—and rewire my brain, train my brain to
Live at home and not in combat anymore.
Help me with the memories and the shame of reaction to
an action
That I was trained to react to save my live and the lives
of others.
Please help me in the flight/fight caveman instinct that
saved my live
And the lives of others but now is floating around in my
mind, not
Really understanding what to do.
Jesus my very being is so wounded help me to focus on
your wounds, PLEASE carry me through this that I
might know that I might know that I might know
that you are slowly healing me from the inside out.
Jesus I put my hand in yours and, even though I might
struggle with trust, I trust you.
You know me
You know when I suffer
You know when I wake up at night from yet another
"Sit rep"
You know my wound, physical and emotional
Please help me. Bring people into my life people on my
side that can help me to heal.
Help me Jesus to know that part of my mind as I ask
you to sort me out.
PLEASE put your hands on the flywheel and heal me.
Thank you Jesus.
Amen.

A Prayer for Addicts

Jesus I confess that I have turned to other crutches to help me to heal.
I confess that I have not turned to you.
I confess that I have used, or am now using,
Alcohol, drugs, cigarettes, food, power, anger, rage,
causing pain to others, angry sex, pornography,
manipulation, and other ways to cope with what I have been through.
I now, by an act of faith, hand over to you those coping mechanisms,
all of them that are not from you.
I give you the things that I am not proud of to help me through the day.
Teach me Lord to reach out to you—that you will help me, guide me and help me
break away from those things that are damaging me.
Jesus help me to trust again.
PLEASE help me to break any addictive behaviors that are
Self-destructive and damaging to those loved ones around me.
Lord I need you.
Lord I want you to set me free.
You came to set the captives free. Please, please set me free
From MY addictions.

A Prayer for Those Considering Suicide

*I've tried everything and nothing helps. I'm at the end
of my rope. Is there no one who can do anything for
me? Isn't that the real question?*

Romans 7:24 (The Message)

Jesus my mind is in chaos.
I have had this nagging thought about ending it.
*I have endured so much I am not sure I can endure
anymore.*
*Please help me NOW. Help me to turn to you for your
divine help.*
*PLEASE help my mind with this constant thought of
self-destruction.*
*I now, by an act of faith, give you all the thoughts and
words spoken and unspoken about just shifting off this
mortal coil. PLEASE help me right now. Right now
Jesus. I really want to take away the pain but not in
this fashion. Jesus what I really want is for you to
take away the pain not into death but into life and life
abundant as YOU promised. PLEASE rewire my mind
and as you died on the cross you took my pain, my
infirmity, my issue, my raw negative life and you gave
me life. PLEASE give that life to me now.*
HELP ME JESUS IN THIS RAW PAIN.
Set me free into life, chase away the shadow of death.
Bring caring people to help me Lord.
Thank you for saving my life.
As I say one word. Jesus.
Amen.

"You're blessed when you're at the end of your rope.
With less of you there is more of God."
Matthew 5:3 (The Message)

A Prayer for the Combat Veteran

In the name of Jesus Christ please help me.
I have seen and experienced man's inhumanity to man
And this experience is affecting me Lord.
Please help me and give me coping skills for daily life.
Help me to be calm and not be stimulated by any form
of violence
Be it a loud noise, a shock or any form of button
pushing.
Help me to love and to be loved.
Help me to forgive.
Help me with any survivor's guilt I may be feeling.
Jesus please rewire my brain that I may not be haunted
by the past.
Guide me into a place of peace and Holy understanding.
Help me to see you standing between me and the enemy.
Jesus help me with the flash backs.
Bring me to a place of healing in my mind and in my
body and in my soul.
Show me, Oh God, how to heal from these unseen
wounds that
Affect and infect my life.
Jesus please come alongside me and teach me how to
again.
I pray for my spouse for patience.
I pray that this uninvited diagnosis will be removed by
You God.

Just as you were awoken in the back of the boat Jesus
I now wake you and ask you to calm the storm in my
mind.
Please stretch out your hand Jesus toward my head and
say your words:
"Peace be still."
Oh God, please bring people chosen by you into my life to
help me
in the process of healing.
Teach me Jesus to be healed of these trauma memories.
Please reframe my mind and put it right within me.
I know with your help all things are possible.
Thank you for your healing grace upon my life.
I believe Lord, help me with my unbelief.
Thank you for Your anointing of my forehead and
Of my trigger finger.
May I truly know that I am welcomed home.
Amen.

A Prayer for Those Who Lost Loved Ones in Combat

Oh God my heart is broken.
The thing I feared has come upon me.
I have lost a loved one in combat.
Jesus I know that you have welcomed them into
your arms
And that they are now at peace.
Please help me with my pure and unadulterated grief.
Help my mind when it goes all over the place in pain.
Help me to grieve well.
Help me through the denial.
Help me through the anger.
Help me through the bargaining.

Help me though the depression.
Help me through the acceptance.
Help me through this very painful grief.
Jesus help me to sleep and if I awaken at night, help me
Through the night as I quietly grieve the loss.
Teach me oh God how to grieve.
I know that you are with me always and that
you will never leave me.
Jesus please stand in the gap between my loved one
and me.
Thank you for your help Jesus.
Amen.

A Prayer for Your Medication

Jesus, for what I am about to receive may I be truly
thankful.
Thank you for gifting, your technology, upon the people
who made this medication and may it hit the target
without any side effects.
I bless, in your most Holy Name, each component and
molecular structure
of this medication and pray that it will be very
effective. I pray for the doctor who prescribed it and the
pharmacist who designed it in your name.
I bless this medication in the name of the Father and of
the Son and of the Holy Spirit. Amen

A Prayer for Peace

Oh God let there be peace on earth and goodwill toward
mankind.

*Oh God please stand between all those of ill will and
those seeking
To cause pain to others with those who are seeking
peace.
Please bring your peace that surpasses all understanding
upon this earth that we have so messed up.
Amen.*

A Welcome Home Prayer

*Jesus, THANK YOU for bringing me home.
I have felt like a prodigal.
Now I am back and trying to fit into "normal" life
again.
It is so good to be home but please help me in this
Transformation from combat to peace. Hundreds have
gone before me I know, hundreds retuning home after
combat. Hundreds feeling exactly what I am feeling but
I do not know what to do.
Please help me Jesus as you welcome me home.
Thank you for sparing my life.
Amen.*

The Last Word

The last words Jesus said,

> *"Father, forgive them, for they do not know
> what they are doing."*
> (Luke 23:34)

Jesus, please take away an unforgiveness that is
festering within me.
Either anything about others or for anything within
myself that I am holding onto. Please take it from me.
Completely.
Take anything that is causing any form
Of emotional Cancer within my very being.
Cleanse my heart, Cleanse my mind, and
Jesus, cleanse my very Soul.
"Just say the Word Lord and I shall be healed."
Heal me Lord of the traumas of the past.
Thank you Jesus.
Amen.

Welcome home my friend
AND
Thank you for serving your country

AMEN

About the Author

Fr. Mumford is the director of the healing ministry at Christ the King, Spiritual Life Center, Greenwich NY with the Episcopal Dioceses of Albany. The ministry has approximately 30 volunteer trained prayer team members.

Fr. Mumford was born and educated in England. He served for six and a half years in Her Majesty's Royal Marine Commandos and continued his education while in the armed forces. His last two years as a Marine were spent as a drill instructor at the Commando Training School (CTCRM).

In 1980, he came to America and set up the Mumford Company Inc., a picture framing business in Wilton and Bethel, Connecticut, which he owned and operated for 13 years. In 1995 he sold his business and has since dedicated his life to the ministry of healing.

His conviction to pray for healing came in 1989 when his sister, Julie Sheldon, a ballet dancer with the Royal Ballet in London, was healed by God through the late Canon Jim Glennon. This was a very dramatic healing from a disease called Dystonia, a neurological condition that curled her up into a fetal position and left her very close to death. Being a witness to her healing has had a profound effect on his life.

Fr. Mumford graduated from Episcopal Training, "The Ministry Exploration and Education Program" (MEEP) in June, 1995, as a lay minister. He was formally installed as the director of the Oratory by the Episcopal Bishop of Connecticut in 1997. He was ordained an Episcopal priest on Dec 17th 2005 with the Episcopal diocese of Albany by The Rt. Rev. Daniel Herzog.

Fr. Mumford is a published author, his publications

include: *Hand to Hand From Combat to Healing* (Church Publishing Inc), (Hand to Hand is available on CD) , *The Forgotten Touch* (Seabury Press).

Also: from Oratory Press: *Heartfelt Prayers For Healing, Thirty One Day Devotional, The Practice of Soaking Prayer, & A Prescription for Healing* . Plus two CD's *Relaxation & Healing Prayer* and *The Essence of Soaking Prayer.*

Fr. Nigel has written a third book expected to be released in Aug. 2011 *After the Trauma the Battle Begins/Post Trauma Healing* / a book on PTSD.

A prayer by Fr. Nigel was published in Race and Prayer Morehouse Publishing Inc. Nigel regularly contributes articles to the quarterly Sharing Magazine (OSL)

The ministry has been reported by the New York Times and two stories of healing have been published in Guideposts Magazine, (Dec 2000 and Feb 2006).

In 2008, A new program was created at the Healing Ministry, called "The Welcome Home Initiative" led by Fr. Nigel, and two other retired military men, Bishop David Bena, and Lt Col. Noel Dawes. This three day retreat program invites men, women & families of our Armed Forces from all wars, who have served in combat, to come "free of charge" and be "welcomed home. " This program provides ministry and resources for health and healing.

In December of 2008, Fr. Mumford had the honor to share The Welcome Home Initiative program, to Army Chaplains with General Douglas Carver at the Pentagon in Washington, DC. In September 2009 in the UK Fr. Nigel had the privilege to speak with General, The Lord Richard Dannet GCB, CBE, MC, DL (Chief of the General Staff, British Army 2006-2009) who was interested about the veterans program.

Fr. Mumford has presented the healing ministry at The Episcopal Cathedrals of Boston MA, Hartford, CT and New York City; Johns Hopkins Hospital, Conference on

"Complementary Medicine". Seminaries: Yale, New Haven, CT, Trinity Seminary, Ambridge, PA, Nashotah House Seminary, WI, Gordon College, Wenham, MA and Wycliffe Hall, Oxford, England. He has preached and led Healing Conferences in many venues throughout the United States. Fr. Nigel has had the privilege to speak in British Colombia, Canada and in the UK: Sussex, Kent and London, Belfast, Northern Ireland & Sweden.

Nigel is a circuit speaker for the International Order of St. Luke. He has been the keynote speaker for the American National OSL and for ACTS/ Associations of Christian Therapists. Fr. Mumford has spoken at the Universities of Cornell, NY. Hobart and William Smith, NY, Hamilton College, NY and Gordon Collage, MA

Fr. Nigel is on the National Advisory Board of Christian Healing Ministries in Jacksonville Florida, (Dr. Francis and Judith MacNutt). He is a member of The Association of Christian Healing Centers in the UK, and has been affiliated with Burrswood, a Christian Hospital in Kent, England. Fr. Mumford is a chaplain and North American Board Member with the International Order of St. Luke.

He is a Paul Harris Fellow from Rotary International and a recipient of The Wittnauer Humanitarian award NY City, 1995.

Fr. Nigel received, inspiration and encouragement from his father the Reverend David Mumford, his uncle Alec McCowen, OBE., CBE. (a renowned English actor), the late Reverend Canon Jim Glennon, Dr. Francis and Judith MacNutt, and the healing of his sister Julie Sheldon; all led to the empowerment of his ministry. He is deeply grateful to them.

In October 2009, Fr. Nigel was hospitalized with H1N1, neumonia and secondary pneumonia and was near death. was in a chemical induced coma for 19 days, after being put on a ventilator. He was then given a tracheotomy. 6 weeks in ICU and 3 weeks at a Rehab facility, Fr. Nigel was sent home on Dec. 23, 2009, to continue his recovery. The pulmonologist told him; "you were as close to death without dying that I have ever seen". Fr. Nigel gives thanks and praise to all the intercessors who lifted him up in prayer, he is alive because of prayer. Thank you Jesus!

Dec. 2010, over a year later, Fr. Nigel has returned to traveling around the world, teaching & preaching the Healing Ministry of Jesus Christ.

Outside the ministry, Fr. Mumford enjoys sailing, boating, swimming, gardening, writing, public speaking, and playing the violin, bagpipes, and clarinet. Fr. Mumford lives with his wife Lynn in Greenwich, near Saratoga Springs, NY.

Fr. Mumford can be reached at:

info@byhiswoundsministry.org
www.byhiswoundsministry.org